The British Army

A CONCISE HISTORY

JOCK HASWELL

The British Army

A CONCISE HISTORY

with 176 illustrations

THAMES AND HUDSON · LONDON

*To soldiers of all ranks, past and present, with thankfulness
and admiration, this book is respectfully dedicated*

Frontispiece: 'Service is Power', an illustration from
The Book of the Army Pageant (1910).

© 1975 Thames and Hudson Ltd, London

Printed in Great Britain by
Jarrold and Sons Ltd, Norwich

CONTENTS

Author's Note

Sir John Fortescue, the great historian of the British army, filled thirteen thick volumes and only got as far as 1870. Much has happened since then. In the basement of the Old War Office Building in Whitehall is a vast library of books about the army.

Therefore this book is rather like the small boy's description of a fishing-net: lots of holes joined together with string. If the string is thin it is because it could be only 40,000 words thick. And since this is, after all, only a single brushline painted across the huge canvas of military history, there is a brief bibliography at the end, intended as a guide for further reading.

Lyminge, 1974   J.H.

Chapter One

THE REGULAR ESTABLISHMENT

Few men have influenced the history and the development of the British army more than Thomas Venner, a wine-cooper and fanatical preacher who kept a clandestine meeting-place for religious dissenters in Coleman Street, in the City of London.

He and his congregation of about thirty 'saints' spent the whole of Sunday, 6 January 1661, preaching, praying and fasting. At about eleven o'clock that night they marched in a body down to St Paul's Churchyard shouting 'Live, King Jesus!' and telling everyone they saw either to join them or stay at home. Grabbing some unfortunate bystander, they killed him when in answer to their questions he told them he was on the side of God and King Charles. The train-bands, called out to arrest the trouble-makers, fled at the sight of them. Venner and his supporters then marched through Aldersgate and spent the night in Cane Wood, between the villages of Hampstead and Highgate.

Very early next morning, General George Monk, the Commander-in-Chief of an army now in the last stages of disbandment, went to the apartments of James, Duke of York, to tell him what had happened. The King, Charles II, was away. He had gone down to Portsmouth a few days before, escorting his mother Henrietta Maria on the first stage of her journey back to France. Monk told James that he had been able to send only a few troopers of his own cavalry regiment, under the command of Sir Philip Howard, to deal with Venner's fanatics, but they were hiding in the depths of the wood where the horsemen could not get at them.

Two days later, at seven o'clock on Tuesday morning, Venner and his misguided Fifth Monarchy Men, who took their title from the forty-fourth verse of the second chapter of the Book of Daniel, emerged from the wood. They stormed through Aldgate announcing their determination to take up arms for 'King Jesus' against the powers of the world, and advanced along Leadenhall, past the Exchange to Woodstreet, where they were confronted by twenty

General George Monk, architect of the Restoration and Commander-in-Chief of Charles II's army.

of Monk's Horse Guards. The train-bands, braver in daylight, came up behind them from Cheapside, and the 'saints', barricading themselves in an ale-house, resolved to fight to the end. James and Monk, hearing that Venner had returned, cantered down to the City with twenty troopers who constituted the whole palace guard. They were met by the Lord Mayor who told them that the 'rebellion' was over. All Venner's men had been either killed or captured. Venner himself was wounded nineteen times and the surgeons complained of the difficulty in keeping him alive long enough to be executed.

It had been a brief, bloody little business, swiftly concluded by the muskets of the train-band and the hangman's rope, but the results were far-reaching. In a country where there was still much support for Oliver Cromwell's form of dictatorship, and the recently restored Stuarts were far from secure, the danger of armed risings suddenly became obvious and urgent. Under the vague terms of the Declaration of Breda Charles II had undertaken to abolish the standing army, and all that was now left of Cromwell's magnificent 'New Model', which had won great victories at Naseby, Dunbar, Preston and Worcester, subdued Ireland and supported the French monarchy on the dunes outside Dunkirk, were the remnants of Monk's own regiments, one of Horse and the other of Foot. Ever since the Restoration, the King's brother James had been advocating the retention of a small, permanent military force for the protection of the King's person, but had been unable to press the point for fear of raising a storm of protest.

Venner's Insurrection halted the disbandment of Monk's regiments. On the morning of 14 February 1661 they paraded on Tower Hill, laid down their arms and, to the immense satisfaction of every man on parade, straightway took them up again in the service of the King, under the titles of the Lord General's Troop of Guards and the Lord General's Regiment of Foot Guards. It was the birthday of the British regular army although no such idea was in the minds of the King or his ministers. They had no intention of creating a standing army. They were merely establishing, on a temporary basis, a reasonably effective system for guarding the King and thus maintaining public order. Yet Monk's Regiment of Foot survives today as the Coldstream Guards.

For centuries the English had had a strong aversion to any form of permanent army, partly because, as an island race, their survival had never been threatened by anything more serious than tribal warfare with the Scots and Welsh. Continental nations depended on an army for their existence; England relied upon her navy, and since she had a naval tradition going back to Alfred the Great her people could see no reason why professional soldiers should be paid to do what had always been managed perfectly well by amateurs ever since the Norman Conquest. Any such institution as a standing army was regarded as entirely unnecessary, and in fact the whole history of the British army reflects this attitude. Completely neglected in peacetime yet expected to achieve miracles in war, the only periods of progress and reform were during or immediately after an emergency when, through no fault of its own, the army had been unable to meet all the demands made on it.

No one had ever disputed the need for soldiers, particularly to satisfy the ambition of bellicose English kings embarking upon continental adventures or to cope with a threatened invasion, and at various times all sorts of different arrangements had been made for calling up able-bodied men at short notice. The primitive national army of the English consisted of the mass of free landowners between the ages of sixteen and sixty, whose term of service was fixed by custom at two months in the year. It was known as the Fyrd. King Alfred reorganized it, divided the country up into military districts and required all landowners with a certain minimum holding of property to do 'thane's service'. This meant they had to provide themselves with their own arms and equipment and serve from the beginning to the end of a campaign.

The first renowned victory of the English army, the Fyrd, was also Alfred the Great's first major battle, at Ashdown on the Berkshire hills in January 871. It became a rout and the corpses of the Danes slaughtered in flight were strewn across the downland as far as Reading.

Canute introduced a new idea when he formed a royal bodyguard of between 3,000 and 6,000 picked troops known as 'house-carles', and it was with a reasonably trained force of house-carles and the raw levies of the Fyrd that Harold fought the two greatest battles in early English history, at Stamford Bridge and Senlac, or Hastings, in 1066. The former was a decisive victory which put an end to the long period of Scandinavian invasions, and the latter a defeat which was nothing like so conclusive as many historians make out. Duke William of Normandy, surnamed the Bastard, certainly won the battle but the conquest of England took him another seven years.

The battle on Senlac ridge was an unpleasant surprise to the Norman knights, for they discovered that the English actually preferred to fight on foot. On the Continent, by contrast, the infantry were regarded as the lowest form of military life: physically, morally and socially far inferior to the mounted men-at-arms who could be of any rank from prince to squire. The battlefield was dominated by the cavalryman, encased in steel and armed with the lance, a weapon he found to be well suited for knocking his social

The climax of the Battle of Hastings. Harold is struck down by a mailed and mounted Norman knight while his house-carles stand firm against cavalry attack.

equals out of their saddles and for spitting the unprotected enemy infantry when they turned and fled. It had been confirmed in many a continental contest that foot soldiers, armed usually with some sort of cutting or stabbing weapon, could not stand up to the lumbering charge of mailed horsemen. If employed as archers or crossbowmen they were not very effective. Their bows were short and the arrows seldom penetrated even a leather jerkin. Crossbows, discharging a heavy bolt or quarrel, had good penetration at short ranges but were cumbersome and difficult to load.

William of Normandy, with three cavalry divisions behind him, looked with scorn on Harold's infantry drawn up along the ridge where Battle Abbey now stands, and the knights and barons behind him were confident that one charge would win the battle. They went forward, and many were swept out of the saddle with their skulls split like firewood by fearful two-handed battle-axes, wielded by strong men who went on wielding them for nine hours on that short October day. The infantry did not break. Even when lured from their commanding height by a feigned retreat, and surrounded in the valley, they fought to the end. When Harold was killed they withdrew in good order and at every ditch, hedge or defile they turned to hammer the pursuing Frenchmen to whom hitherto the chasing of infantry had been the most amusing and enjoyable aspect of war. So many Normans died unpleasantly in the cold light of the full moon that all thoughts of pursuit were soon abandoned.

The Normans brought in the feudal system, Henry II reorganized it in his Assize of Arms, and Edward I refined it in his Second Statute of Winchester in 1285. This provided a national force of amateur soldiers for home defence which, under such names as train-bands, militia, fencibles and volunteers, remained unaltered in principle until the eighteenth century. The English armies which fought on the Continent in the Middle Ages were raised only for specific campaigns and were disbanded either when they were no longer needed or when there was no more money to pay the soldiers. They contained men who lived by the sword and could therefore be rated as professionals; but there was no military structure or staff, and little attempt was made to delegate the functions of command below the level of commander-in-chief. Supreme command was vested in the king who might, as for example in the case of Edward III and the Black Prince in the Poitiers campaign, appoint a deputy to act in his stead.

Before the days of the longbow, tactics were comparatively simple. Armies either advanced to meet each other, or one stood on the defensive while the other launched a frontal attack. Having no effective projectile, soldiers relied mainly on 'staff' weapons: cutting and stabbing 'heads' mounted on a long staff, such as the partisan, halberd, glaive and pole-axe, with which they hoped to keep the enemy at a reasonable distance. The men-at-arms who were mounted charged with the lance and then used swords and

Early eighteenth-century partisan (*above*) and halberd (*below*), 'staff' weapons which had changed little since their introduction in the Middle Ages.

The code of chivalry laid stress on the personal encounter between social equals. In this representation, Richard the Lionheart tilts against Saladin.

maces when they closed with the enemy. Battles usually became a mêlée of close-quarter fighting, little more than indiscriminate hacking and bashing which went on until one side felt it had had enough. The knights and nobility did not expect to get killed because if unhorsed by an opponent – and from their point of view battle was only a continuation of the tilting-yard – a knight who was clearly at a disadvantage would surrender and be ransomed. Only the common soldiers – the infantry – suffered.

Then Edward I, in his attempts to comb the Welsh out of their tangled hills, discovered the longbow of Gwent, the weapon which, for range, penetration, rate of fire, accuracy and general handiness, was unequalled until the invention of the modern rifle. As a long-range weapon the longbow virtually put an end to the personal combat between knights that was the essence of the chivalric code of honour. The terrible arrow-storms at Crécy (1346), Poitiers

A stylized version of the Battle of Crécy (1346) illustrating Froissart's Chronicles. It shows the Genoese crossbowmen in conflict with English and Welsh archers, and, in the margin, the early 'bombard'.

Siege warfare: the reduction of an English-held town in France by the siege-train of the Bureau brothers.

(1356) and Agincourt (1415) established the salient fact that cavalry could not make any headway against the archer who stood behind a protective entanglement of sharpened stakes linked with strong cord, sending his cloth-yard shafts hissing through the air to kill men and horses at a range of nearly a quarter of a mile. Backed up by men-at-arms to protect him when he had discharged his quiverful of twenty-four arrows, and by cavalry to exploit the arrow-storm, the longbowman was a formidable opponent.

Artillery, although employed in the form of light field-pieces at Crécy, was first developed as an offensive and supporting weapon in France, in the third decade of the fifteenth century, by the brothers Bureau. It was not popular at first: no one could be quite sure whether the shot would emerge from the proper end, as everyone hoped, or whether the gun would explode like a monster grenade and slay the crew. But the effect of bombards and cannon on siege warfare was considerable, for breaches in walls could be made and stormed without waiting for garrisons to be starved into surrender. And in open warfare guns carefully sited to take advancing infantry in enfilade could create excellent opportunities for one's own cavalry.

The greater range of the cannon made the longbow obsolete. Instead, a new weapon – the matchlock harquebus, based on the

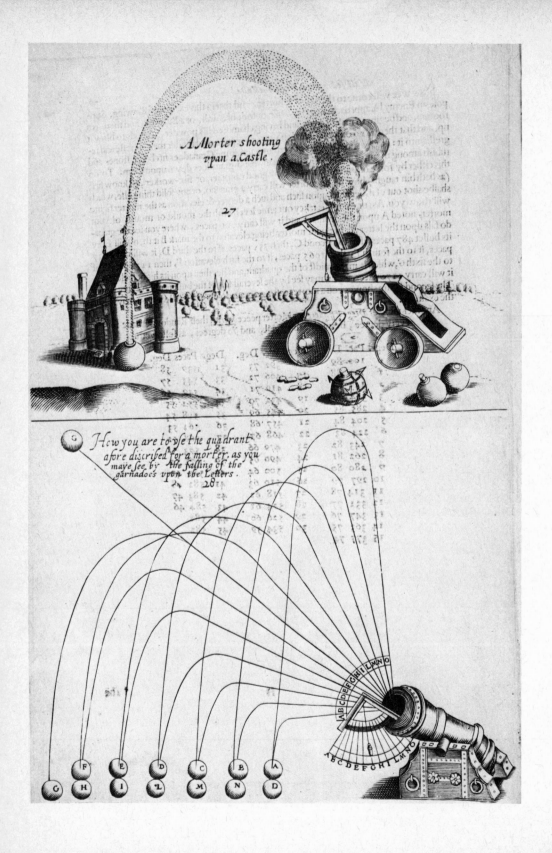

A Morter shooting
vpan a Castle.

27

How you are to vse the quadrant
afore discribed for a morter, as you
maye see by the falling of the
garnadoes vpon the Letters.
28

principles of the cannon – was produced for the infantry; but, for many years, what one chronicler described with considerable exaggeration as 'the fatal discharge' was nothing of the sort. The harquebus was extremely inaccurate and even light armour such as the breastplate gave good protection against the comparatively slow-moving bullet.

When gunpowder replaced the bowstring as a means of propulsion the infantry's rate of fire dropped from a maximum of some fifteen arrows a minute to one soft lead bullet every quarter of an hour – if the operator of the harquebus was reasonably well trained and nothing went wrong. This was because the loading and priming of weapons involved thirty separate drill movements controlled by an officer who gave the necessary orders. In the long pauses between each round fired, the musketeers could take no active part in a battle and had to be protected by pikemen, who were armed with weapons eighteen feet long to hold off enemy cavalry. Since the effective range of the flintlock musket – which superseded the harquebus – was between fifty and eighty yards, depending on the amount of powder behind the bullet, cavalry once more asserted themselves. Hence the dictum of Oliver Cromwell that 'the best military weapon is a man on a horse'.

Infantry, therefore, consisted of musketeers and pikemen, an inseparable combination until the invention of the bayonet, and their function was to get within musket shot of the enemy and shoot them down. The role of cavalry was to drive the enemy's Horse from the field and then ride down their pikemen, automatically putting the musketeers to flight. All this was nothing like so easy as it sounds, and one hazard, often overlooked in any discussion of the tactics of this period, was smoke. Depending on the strength of the wind, battlefields were usually shrouded in a thick, choking pall of smoke from the black powder used in every firearm, and until the invention of smokeless powder towards the end of the nineteenth

A manual of cavalry tactics. Note the use of harquebuses on the left.

Opposite: artillery fire has always been a matter more of geometry than mathematics. A page from a military handbook published in 1639.

15

PAINTED GLASS
IN A
WINDOW
OF
FARNDON CHURCH
Containing Portraits
of Cheshire Gentlemen
who attended K.Charles I.
at the Siege of Chester.

From a Drawing contributed by
the very Rev.ᵈ Hugh Cholmondeley
Dean of Chester.

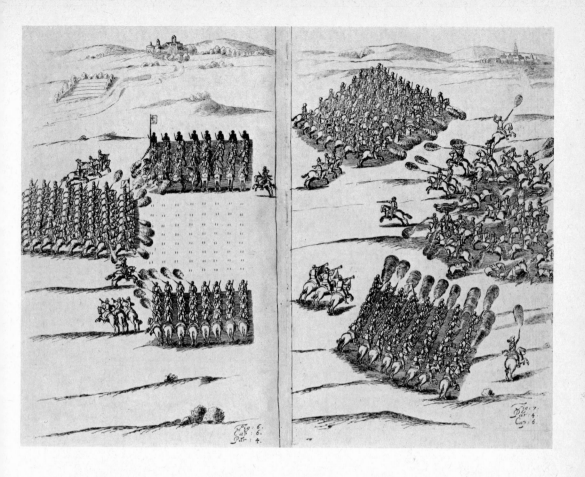

century it was almost impossible for a soldier to see the effect of his fire or for a commander to see what was happening, unless he kept well back from the fight.

Horsemen could only succeed against pikemen by breaking the infantry's formation, so infantry tactics became a matter of close-formation drills designed to ensure that foot soldiers were never caught unawares by cavalry in the open. Although the rebellious American Colonists of the 1770s taught the British redcoats not to bunch too tightly, it was not until the Boer War of 1899 that the infantry really shook out into open order.

The English armies which fought against the French and Spanish in the sixteenth and early seventeenth centuries consisted, like their medieval counterparts, of irregular troops who were paid off at the close of a campaign. Cromwell's New Model Army, founded in 1645, was the first national force to be made up of regulars: it became a standing army during his lifetime, and his son Richard would no doubt have maintained it had he been given the opportunity. Cromwell fully appreciated the principle later expressed in Mao Tse-tung's aphorism 'political power grows out of the barrel

Cavalry, like infantry, appreciated the importance of 'keeping formation'. Illustrations from *Militarie Instructions for the Cavallrie* by John Cruso (1632).

Opposite: Royalist troops and weapons of the Civil War. Among the weapons and equipment illustrated are the matchlock and ramrod, the musketeer's bandolier and cartridge pouches, and swords, pikes and halberds.

of a gun', and his Ironsides and his Major-Generals retained so firm a hold on the country that they became, in the words of a contemporary, 'An Aweful Warning' of the evils inherent in a permanent force. Future generations of politicians were to quote the 'Rule of the Major-Generals' as the unanswerable political argument against a regular army, although in fact they were usually only expressing their refusal to pay for one.

Against this background, and after the initial euphoria of the Restoration had begun to evaporate, Charles II had to move carefully. Though perhaps one of the laziest he was also one of the most astute politicians in English history, and he thoroughly understood the people he ruled. He made no attempt to create a standing army and thus there is no definite and indisputable date for its creation. It evolved gradually, remaining unacknowledged for many years

Oliver Cromwell, the commander who was convinced that 'the best military weapon is a man on a horse'.

OLIVARIVS CROMWELL EXERCITVVM ANGLIÆ TENENS ET GVBERNATOR HIBERNIÆ OXO

REIPVBLICÆ DVX GENERALIS LOCVM-NIENSIS ACADEMIÆ CANCELLARIVS

Charles II.

after it had come into existence. There is a political parallel in the development of the British Cabinet system.

To comply with an Act of Parliament the remnants of Cromwell's Ironsides had to be formally disbanded – hence the parade on Tower Hill – but in their place the force to protect the King was considerably increased. In addition to Monk's renamed Regiment of Foot there was a 'new' regiment of twelve companies of Guards, commanded by Colonel John Russell. This in effect consisted of men who had served Charles and James during their exile, and many of them had fought on the Royalist side in the Civil War. As a royal regiment they took precedence over the Coldstream.

The King's troop of Horse Guards, and James's own troop that he had commanded in France and the Low Countries, combined to become a Regiment of Horse with eight troops, commanded by the

An officer of the 'Tangiers Regiment' (2nd of Foot) on active service in Tangier, 1669.

Earl of Oxford. This took precedence over Monk's cavalry regiment, and the two regiments became known as the First and Second Regiments of Life Guards. From the colour of its uniforms Lord Oxford's regiment became known as 'The Blues'.

This royal bodyguard of cavalry and infantry was still not large enough to satisfy those ardent monarchists who feared a repetition of Venner's Insurrection, and in 1662 Douglas's Regiment, which had been part of the Scots Brigade of Gustavus Adolphus, King of Sweden, was brought back to England from garrison duties at Dunkirk. It was granted precedence over the regiment raised by Lord Peterborough in 1661 to defend Queen Catherine of Braganza's dowry port of Tangier, largely because in one form or another it had been fighting in continental wars for nearly a century. These two regiments became the 1st and 2nd of Foot (as opposed to Foot Guards). The former still exists as The Royal Scots whereas the latter, first placed on the establishment as 'Our Most Dear Consort the Queen's Regiment of Foot' and subsequently better known as the Queen's Royal Regiment, amalgamated with the East Surrey Regiment in 1960, only a few months before its tercentenary.

To those who became uneasy about this marked increase in the military establishment Charles could point out what most people realized. None of the regiments was 'new', except for The Queen's, which had been raised solely for garrison duties overseas, and provided employment for 1,000 demobilized and destitute men who had served in Cromwell's army.

The alliance with Portugal, through Catherine of Braganza, gave Charles's army its first experience of colonial warfare, for garrisons had to be sent to protect the dowry ports of Tangier and Bombay. The Portuguese were not in the least reluctant to part with Tangier. The anchorage was unsafe for shipping and round the massive fortifications on the landward side roamed the savage Moors who never missed an opportunity to harass the garrison. After twenty-three years of incessant warfare, in which young John Churchill, later the first Duke of Marlborough, gained his first experience of active service with The Queen's, the place was evacuated in 1684. Bombay was a different proposition altogether, being a gateway to the riches of the East. When Sir Abraham Shipman and 400 troops arrived there in 1662 they were not allowed to land because no decision had been taken on what constituted the ill-defined area of Bombay. By March 1665, when the Portuguese at last moved out, the British contingent had been reduced by sickness and death to one officer and 113 men. As the opening moves in the acquisition of the British Empire neither of these adventures was much of a success.

James, Duke of York, succeeded his brother and becames James II in 1685. From the beginning this soldier and sailor king was politically out of his depth, and his flat statement to the Commons that he wanted 'a good force of well-disciplined troops in constant pay' (justified by the signal failure of the West Country militia to

S. Moore fe.

A. Whitehall.   C Irish battery E York Castle G Charles F. I Whitby   L Tiveot slain May 16.1564
B. Bridges   D Platharin   F Upper Ca: H Henrietta K Moores T. M The Moores Ambasead of Horse

cope with Monmouth's Rebellion) was interpreted as a threat of arbitrary rule. Nevertheless James went much further than Charles had ever dared. In the first year of his brief reign nine regiments of infantry, five of Horse and two of dragoons (mounted infantry) were raised, ostensibly to deal with any aftermath of the Duke of Argyll's abortive rising in Scotland and Monmouth's efforts, brought to nothing at Sedgemoor. But the new regiments remained in being, concentrated in a field army based on the permanent camp on Hounslow Heath, even after the revolts had been crushed.

James was a first-class administrator. Fortescue, the army's greatest historian whose praise for administrators is sparing, wrote, 'it is not too much to say that his expulsion was in this respect the greatest misfortune that ever befell the Army.' As Lord High Admiral in his brother's reign he had, with the help of Samuel Pepys, built the foundations of the Royal Navy. Now, because soldiering was his first love, he brought the army under his personal command, sponsored a new drill-book and introduced new training methods practised in proper training camps. The isolated detachments in garrisons and fortresses were grouped in regiments and for the first time the whole army came under the influence of methodical administration.

The Port of Tangier which, with Bombay, formed part of the dowry of Catherine of Braganza, wife of Charles II. These were the first overseas garrisons of the British regular army.

By the year 1688 James had a standing army of more than 34,000 men, paid for by the simple expedient of diverting funds allocated by Parliament to the militia. Thus it can be said that he was the true founder of the regular army, which dates from the period 1685–8.

Unfortunately James was a Roman Catholic commanding an army which was overwhelmingly Protestant, and his attempts to infiltrate a leavening of Roman Catholic officers were bitterly resented and contributed to his downfall. His son-in-law, William of Orange, married to his eldest daughter Mary, offered an alternative and Protestant succession. In November 1688 William and a small Dutch force landed at Torbay. The principal officers of James's army, including Lieutenant-General Churchill, deserted to the enemy, and without their officers the rank and file loyal to James could do little to support him.

High on the list of James's alleged misdemeanours was the charge of 'raising and keeping a Standing Army within this Kingdom in time of Peace without consent of Parliament and Quartering Soldiers contrary to Law'. Attitudes had not changed since the fall of Charles II's faithful minister Edward Hyde, Lord Clarendon, in 1667. The first article in his impeachment claimed that he had 'designed a Standing Army to be Raised, and to govern the Kingdom thereby'. Military power was in no way compatible with political freedom. A standing army was the symbol of arbitrary rule. James had lost his throne because he proved this to be true, and in so doing he had given the country an unpleasant fright, aggravated by the 'Aweful Warning' across the Channel where the absolute monarchy of his cousin Louis XIV was supported by the largest army in Europe.

James II (*above*), founder of the regular army shown drawn up (*below*) on the permanent camp on Hounslow Heath in 1686.

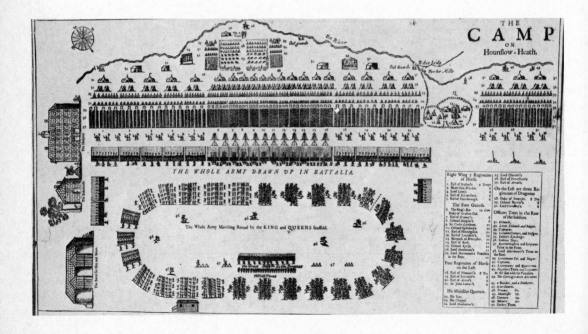

Infantrymen of the Second Queen's in 1687: a pikeman, a grenadier and a musketeer.

The deep-rooted antipathy to a permanent army made things very awkward for the new King, William III, whose decision to intervene in England had been greatly influenced by the thought that he would be able to add the armed forces of England to his coalition against Louis XIV. British ministers were resolved to prevent any repetition of James's arbitrary government by abolishing the standing army he had raised. To their minds the solution to the political problem was simple enough: there would be no army in peacetime. But this was not peacetime. The activities of Louis XIV all through the year 1688 and his determination to secure the north-eastern frontier of France – in the area of the Low Countries which had been in dispute since the reign of Louis XI – were dragging all Europe into war. Far from being able to disband James's army, the reluctant politicians were compelled to enlarge it.

The Dutch declared war on France in February 1689. In March, James II and a small French army landed in Ireland where Catholic 'rebels' now held most of the country. William sent Marshal Schomberg, now over eighty, to cope with the situation in Ireland

The Battle of the Boyne, 1689: William III's army crossing the river which, as Macaulay wrote, 'was alive with musquets and green boughs'. William's men wore sprigs of green in their hats to distinguish them from James's troops.

while he made preparations for a continental war. In May, William brought the three kingdoms of England, Scotland and Ireland into the war against Louis, and in June of the following year he went over to Ireland and assumed responsibility for the campaign. James, disturbed by William's personal intervention, moved his headquarters from Castle Town and fell back towards Dublin. He crossed the River Boyne on 28 June and camped with his army near the bridge. Two days later William followed up, halted when he reached the Boyne and drew up his army in two lines facing the

river. His feint frontal attack and massive right hook over the Slane
Bridge, two miles up-river, were entirely successful. James returned
to France, and since Schomberg had been killed in the Battle of the
Boyne, William left his Dutch General Ginkel to complete what he
described as 'the entire Reducing of Ireland' – which Ginkel did, by
September 1691.

Feeling free now to give his full attention to the war in Europe,
William sent troops to Flanders, but had to recall many of them
hastily when James took command of an invasion force of 20,000

French regular troops and Irish volunteers which had assembled near Cherbourg. An Anglo-Dutch fleet under Admirals Russell and van Almonde put an end to all James's hopes at the battle off Cap la Hogue in May 1692.

In his continental campaigns William III showed himself to be an enthusiastic soldier but a disappointing general with very little administrative ability. It is true that he was greatly outnumbered by the French – by as much as two to one in cavalry, the decisive arm. But though his strategy in trying to force the French to fight at a disadvantage was sound enough, he lacked the tactical skill to exploit it. He was thoroughly defeated by the French Marshal Luxembourg at Steinkirk in 1692 and Landen in the following year. Luxembourg died during the winter of 1694, and in 1695 William gained his only success with the capture of the great fortress of Namur, defended by Marshal Boufflers. Even so, the British suffered 9,000 casualties against French losses of 6,500. The last two campaigns of King William's War – also known as the 'War of the League of Augsburg' – were indecisive, and fighting ended when the Treaty of Ryswick was signed in 1697.

As Stadtholder of the Netherlands, William had been at war with Louis XIV ever since 1672 and though there was little enough to show for his campaigns he had succeeded in exhausting his far more powerful opponent. France was desperately short of money and Louis was almost at the end of his resources, yet the peace was no more than an uneasy truce and a prelude to the War of the Spanish Succession.

Britain, led by a Dutchman into the war against France, had in fact entered upon a second Hundred Years War against her traditional enemy, a war differing radically from all the others she had fought. It was a struggle to decide which nation would own an empire that would dominate the world. It was fought in four main areas of conflict, Europe, North America, India and the Caribbean, largely by men recruited, trained and paid as regular soldiers of a professional army. It was conducted by generals who were professional soldiers. The era of the warrior kings had passed, although George II awoke the echoes of it when he commanded the army at Dettingen in 1743. Henceforth the story of the army is punctuated with the names of the great captains: Marlborough (whose debt to William's war of attrition is seldom acknowledged), Amherst, Wellington, Roberts, Wolseley, Kitchener and the field-marshals of the twentieth century.

Chapter Two

THE ACQUISITION OF EMPIRE

In the latter part of the seventeenth century France, politically and militarily, was the greatest power in Europe. Louis II de Bourbon, better known as the Prince de Condé or Le Grand Condé, had established the superiority of French arms by his victory over the hitherto 'invincible' Spaniards at the Battle of Rocroi in 1643, and other nations, particularly the Prussians, Austrians and British, were quick to adopt French ideas. One of these was the bayonet, first used in 1647 in France and first issued to a British regiment – the 2nd Foot in Tangier – in 1663. It turned every musketeer into a pikeman – of a sort – but the early pattern plugged into the muzzle of the musket, so the weapon could not be fired. In 1697 a 'socket' bayonet, which locked on the outside of the barrel and could be easily fixed and unfixed, overcame this major disadvantage. By 1705 the pike

The musket with socket bayonet gave the infantryman a dual-purpose weapon, and eventually replaced the pike altogether.

was obsolete although it did not disappear for many years; in 1798, for example, the Irish rebels issued instructions that those armed with pikes were to have 'a yard and a half of green serge hanging to each': one of the origins of 'the wearin' o' the green'.

By 1700, greased paper cartridges carried in pouches had replaced the powder-horn and bandolier, and well-trained musketeers could fire one shot a minute. This increase in the rate of fire led to new tactics in which the British infantry, fighting in three ranks (the front rank kneeling), concentrated in a single firing line with gaps of only two or three paces between battalions. So that shooting should be as continuous as possible, volleys were fired by platoons in a set order. Commanders moved their battalions about the battlefield like unwieldy chessmen, and their object was to present as long a firing line as possible to the enemy, keeping their reserve units close up behind to strengthen any weakening point, replace casualties and prevent the enemy from turning the flanks. Cavalry, because of their mobility and powerful physical impact on stationary bodies of infantry, remained the dominant arm. The continental Horse relied on pistol-fire, the British charged 'knee to knee' with the heavy sabre, and though given a firearm for local protection while their horses were grazing, British troopers were not supposed to use them in action. Marlborough provided his cavalry with breastplates for protection against the enemy's small-arms and issued only three rounds per man for each campaign.

Though Louis XIV's minister the Marquis de Louvois had done his best to abolish the system of trafficking in commissions, which turned French regiments into private businesses run by the officers for their own profit, the roots ran too deep for one man to pull up. William III had no success either, when he attacked the same system

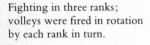

Fighting in three ranks; volleys were fired in rotation by each rank in turn.

in England. The trouble was that the purchase of commissions and promotion was so attractive, financially, to politicians and taxpayers, and was so generally accepted by the officers who benefited by it, that it became a fixed institution. Since officers derived their main income from illicit dealings in food, clothing and equipment, at the expense of their men, it was unnecessary for the taxpayer to provide more than purely nominal salaries. From an officer's point of view, a military career was a commercial enterprise. Promotion was bought and sold, and thus rank and responsibility became entirely separated from ability and experience. Any rich father could buy a commission in a regiment for an infant son. The system led inevitably to a lack of professionalism which degraded the whole army and persisted into the twentieth century. For years the functions of an officer in action were summed up as 'an ability to die gallantly in front of his men'. No other military qualification was necessary, and as a result the majority of officers led their men into battle without even such elementary knowledge as the range of their weapons. Fortunately the competence of their non-commissioned officers and the discipline of their men compensated for these failings.

In the reign of William III the pay of a soldier was two shillings and sixpence a day for a cavalry trooper, one shilling and sixpence for a dragoon and eightpence for a private soldier of a Line regiment. Out of this a man had to feed himself and his horse. A deduction of one shilling in the pound was made for the upkeep of Chelsea Hospital, and gradually all sorts of extra deductions became accepted. Payment for rations in the field, tithes, medicines, payments to regimental auditors and the Paymaster-General were some of the charges invented by regimental colonels to defraud the men under their command. Furthermore the Paymaster-General delayed his payments to regiments sometimes for years and then settled the accounts with such things as tallies and debentures worth only a small fraction of the money due.

Chelsea Hospital, built by Sir Christopher Wren on land obtained by Nell Gwynne who saw the need for a combined hospital and home for disabled and pensioned soldiers. It was the counterpart of Les Invalides in Paris.

However, to the soldier of the post-Restoration years all this was not quite so bad as it may sound. He had probably joined the army as an alternative to starvation or imprisonment. He may have been sent to the army to make room for other prisoners in a gaol. Soldiering to him meant free food and lodging in the house of some citizen, perhaps with a wife and daughter to be enjoyed: a life of comparative idleness and few irksome regulations. He was even given a weapon to support any demands he chose to make on his unwilling host. To such men payment was a bonus. But this state of affairs did not last long. The fierce discipline in the French army, imposed by men such as General Martinet, appealed to William III. Flogging and such punishments as 'the Horse' – the victim was made to sit astride the apex of two boards at a sharp angle, sometimes for several hours and with muskets tied to his ankles – introduced into the army a tradition of brutality that clouds its history for the next 150 years.

Oliver Cromwell's New Model Army had consisted of independently minded fanatical Puritans imbued with self-discipline. Instead of the usual off-duty occupations of a soldier they had been wont to discuss the Scriptures with their officers, sing Psalms and pray. Convinced that they were the instruments of God, they had been superb soldiers, but this sense of dedication did not survive. Officers grew rich by property speculation, dealing in the confiscated estates of Cavaliers and conquered lands in Ireland, and this broke the bonds of fellowship. Mammon became more attractive than God. The pay of the men fell into arrears and in due course the New Model reached the stage where its loyalty and effectiveness depended on one man, the Lord Protector Cromwell.

On his death the religious element melted away. Soldiers were no longer the 'saints' they had been in the great days of 1647, and though recruits for Charles II's regiments had to provide 'testimonies of courage and fidelity' such certificates could be bought easily enough. The quality of soldiers declined rapidly. Recruiting, by 'beat of Drum', developed into kidnapping and depots became indistinguishable from prisons, yet there was no conscription. The system remained 'voluntary' because no British Parliament was prepared to create a large British army. Naturally, in an army in which every form of corruption was rife, in which men were cheated of their pay, starved and often barefoot and in rags, and in which the punishments were barbarous and inhuman, the standard of 'volunteers' fell lower and lower.

Cromwell's Ironsides had been men of considerable social standing, respected figures in the community. Only a few years after the parade on Tower Hill in 1661 this status had been lost. The soldier was not respected, nor did he earn a respectable wage. For a man to join the army – to 'go for a soldier' in the contemporary phrase – was the ultimate failure, a disgrace only one degree above prison, and soldiering as a career sank to the bottom of the social

A life-size 'cut-out' figure of a grenadier of the Queen's Royal Regiment, c. 1715. Figures such as this, displayed outside inns, advertised the presence of a recruiting party.

scale where it remained until the First World War. Not until then, when the whole nation was caught up in war, did 'respectable citizens' go willingly into the ranks of the army.

William III made billeting in private houses illegal, and men were quartered in inns, barns, stables and 'all houses selling brandy and strong waters'. This further reduced the status of soldiering and was no help to discipline.

In 1689 troops earmarked for the campaign in Flanders refused to embark. The politicians were compelled to realize that there were military offences outside the scope of common law, such as mutiny, desertion and sedition, and they hurriedly passed the first Mutiny Act, to be effective for one year only, which authorized execution as the most severe penalty for these crimes. In various forms the Act was passed annually until 1879 and was then embodied in the Army Act of 1881.

Louvois built barracks for Louis XIV's army (the word *barraque* meaning a hut or temporary shelter), but until the end of Anne's reign there were none in England. Troops not accommodated in barns or inns lived in forts or castles such as those at Sissinghurst, Dover and Deal, or in permanent garrisons such as Horse Guards.

A hypothetical picture of Oliver Cromwell preaching to a Puritan congregation after the Battle of Worcester, 1651. Though lucid on paper, he was a bad speaker.

Anno Primo

WILLIELMI & MARIÆ.

An Act for punishing Officers or Souldiers who shall Mutiny or Desert Their Majesties Service.

Whereas the raising or keeping a Standing Army within this Kingdom in time of Peace, unless it be with Consent of Parliament, is against Law; And whereas it is judged necessary by Their Majesties and this present Parliament, That during this time of Danger several of the Forces which are now on foot should be continued, and others raised for the Safety of the Kingdom, for the Common Defence of the Protestant Religion, and for the reducing of Ireland;

S ſ 2   And

Charles II of Spain, who had been lingering on the threshhold of death for some thirty years, died in 1700; there were two claimants for his throne, Louis XIV's grandson, Philip, Duke of Anjou, and Archduke Charles of Austria. William III, ever on guard to check the growth of Catholic power in Europe, had in 1699 negotiated with Louis a Treaty of Partition which made Archduke Charles heir to the Spanish throne, but on his death-bed Charles of Spain signed a will leaving his throne to the Duke of Anjou. Forced to choose between the will and the treaty, Louis chose the will and prepared to defend his grandson's claim.

In the five years since the Treaty of Ryswick the Commons had done their worst with William's army, reducing it from 87,000 to 7,000 men, and so strong was the anti-war feeling that William apparently had no alternative but to acknowledge the Duke of Anjou as King of Spain. But even the House of Commons could see that Protestant Europe might be overwhelmed by the Catholic alliance of France and Spain. The money and men William asked for were voted and at the end of August 1701 England, Holland and Austria formed the nucleus of the Grand Alliance against France.

Half-way through the following month, James II died in exile in the Château of Saint Germain-en-Laye, and Louis, repudiating the clause in the Treaty of Ryswick in which he recognized William as King of England, announced his support for James's son as the rightful James III. This caused considerable irritation among the Whigs in England, and while the drums were beating for more recruits to swell the ranks of the regiments, King William died. Queen Anne, James II's daughter, ascended the throne, bringing with her John Churchill, later to become one of the greatest commanders of all time. Although he raised his country to the status of a great military power, Britain did not become a military state under an absolute monarchy, like France and Prussia. Her powerful army had no political significance.

In the War of the Spanish Succession there were two main theatres: northern and central Europe where the Duke of Marlborough was the Commander-in-Chief; and Spain, where the Allied army, containing Dutch, Portuguese, Germans and Huguenots, was commanded first by Lord Peterborough and then by Henri de Massue, Marquis de Ruvigny, a French Huguenot who had been created Earl of Galway. The Spanish campaign ended in disaster. In 1707 James, Duke of Berwick, who was the bastard son of James II by Arabella Churchill, Marlborough's sister, commanded the combined French and Spanish army. He routed Lord Galway at the Battle of Almanza, where the sudden flight of the Portuguese left the British right flank exposed to the French cavalry, and inflicted 7,000 casualties.

In Europe, Marlborough's great march of 250 miles from Flanders to the Danube in the summer of 1704 illustrated his genius for administration at a time when the problems of moving large forces

Opposite: the first page of the Mutiny Act, 1689.

33

A fanciful view of the capture of Gibraltar in 1704.

over long distances had not been studied in detail. It was in this year that Gibraltar was taken from the Spanish.

Marlborough's skill as a strategist, tactician, diplomat and leader of men was immaculate. His troops, benefiting from his forward planning and always aware of the care he took of them, called him 'Corporal John'. His great victories at Blenheim in August 1704, Ramillies in May 1706, Oudenarde in July and the capture of Lille in October 1708, followed by Malplaquet in September 1709, illustrated his supreme ability to outwit and outmanœuvre his enemies and build success upon success. He never lost an engagement and never failed to take a town he besieged. Malplaquet, his last great battle, was the bloodiest of the century; a total of 36,000 men were killed or wounded. There was no greater slaughter until Napoleon's victory at Borodino, 103 years later.

To the exhaustion of all involved, the war dragged on until 1713, although the new Tory government elected in 1710 was determined to dismiss Marlborough and end the war unilaterally, even at the expense of Britain's allies. Marlborough was replaced in 1712, but the Treaty of Utrecht reflects the scale of his achievements. For eighty years, France, the largest nation in Europe, had been virtually all-powerful on the Continent, but the crippling damage done to her, socially and economically, by Marlborough's victories and the defeat of Louis XIV, can be traced through the dynastic and colonial wars of the eighteenth century down to the French Revolution and the fall of the French monarchy.

Opposite: Kneller's portrait of John Churchill, First Duke of Marlborough, 'trampling War underfoot and crowned by Victory'.

Marlborough's 'famous
victory' of Blenheim in 1704,
illustrating the tight-packed
formations of infantry and
cavalry in the 'chequer-
board' tactics of European
warfare.

It was now England and not France who could determine and adjust the balance of power in Europe. But the Tories, who in opposition had always been against the employment of large British forces in continental coalition armies, were of the opinion that in future wars a 'maritime' strategy, in which combined naval and military expeditions carried the war to the enemy's coast and colonies, would be less expensive and far more effective. They took no account of the appalling wastage of men and horses in movement by sea, for conditions had not improved since the days of Elizabeth I, and the transports used to carry troops during this period have been described as 'floating slaughter-houses'. On any voyage, even

An eighteenth-century field hospital. The patient undergoing an operation was usually made too drunk to care what was happening. When no spirits were available, he was given a bullet to bite on, to prevent his screaming.

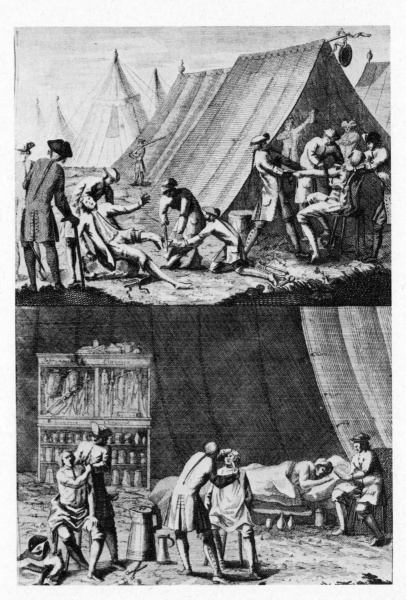

comparatively short ones in European waters, death from such diseases as smallpox, the 'bloody flux' which was dysentery, typhoid fever, pneumonia and tuberculosis usually accounted for between 50 and 60 per cent of any draft. In the West Indies, yellow fever, known as the 'black vomit', on many occasions reduced the ten companies of an infantry battalion to one company's strength in less than a year. Medical services were 'organized' on a regimental basis, in that one possibly unqualified 'surgeon' or 'assistant surgeon' was appointed and paid by the colonel but not provided with any nursing facilities, or drugs and dressings. Confronted with an epidemic on a ship or a heavy casualty-list after a battle, the surgeon could not cope, nor did many of them try. A wounded man was fortunate if he had some female camp-follower to look for him on a battlefield and find him before he was stripped by local peasants and left to die of exposure. In any case the soft lead bullet from a musket caused fearful injuries and few wounded men survived.

In principle the Tories disliked large armies and they hastened to disband Marlborough's forces even before the Treaty of Utrecht had been signed. Thirteen regiments of dragoons and twenty-two of

An infantry regiment on the line of march in 1745, moving to Scotland to help deal with the problems raised by Bonnie Prince Charlie, the Young Pretender. The picture demonstrates the low opinion civilians had of the army.

1 Join your Right Hand to your Firelock

2 Poife your Firelock

3 Join your Left Hand to your Firelock

infantry were removed from the establishment. In 1714, the year after the signing of the treaty, the total strength was fixed at 22,000 men. This included the Irish establishment, the regiments in North America and the West Indies, and those still needed as garrison troops in Flanders. The Jacobite Rising of 1715 checked temporarily the process of reduction, but by 1739 the establishment was down to 18,000, dangerously low in comparison with the French army of 133,000, which would have been even larger but for the poverty of France after Louis XIV's ruinous wars.

Under the House of Hanover the strong, centralized governmental organization inherited from the Tudor and Stuart dynasties gradually gave way to one in which power devolved on the county aristocracy and gentry who, absorbed in local affairs and growing rich from enclosed lands and buoyant overseas trade, had no interest in military matters of any sort. Even the militia, the direct responsibility of the gentlemen of the counties and the only acceptable means of enforcing and supporting local authority, became virtually extinct in all but name. Contingents were not mustered and so remained untrained. The regular army, recruited from criminals, debtors and wastrels, who were robbed and exploited and lived the sort of life from which the only escape, albeit a temporary one, was drunkenness, became especially unpopular – particularly in the towns. Class distinctions were eroding the social structure, and in this age of violence men were prone to make their own adjustments between themselves and the rich. Since there was no police force, the unhappy

THE CITIES OF LONDON | AND WESTMINSTER | This PRINT of the MANUAL

4 Cock your Firelock. | 5 Present. ——— 6 Fire. | 7 Recover your Arms *see fig. 12*
8 Halfcock your Firelock

redcoat became the government's instrument for quelling riots, by force. Soldiers were also made to take action against smugglers, whose activities received the whole-hearted approval of the large majority of people in coastal communities. Altogether, there was little understanding and less goodwill between the public and the army. Yet, by the middle of the eighteenth century the continued existence of a standing army was at last generally though grudgingly accepted, which was just as well since the country soon became involved in a series of protracted wars in North America, India and Europe.

It was unfortunate that just at this time the influence of Prussian military ideas, applicable only to the chequer-board patterns of European warfare, superseded those of France and were given much weight in England. They seemed to work well enough in India, against native levies reluctant to face well-arranged musketry, but they were very nearly fatal to the British cause in North America, although this was largely the fault of individual officers who felt themselves bound by the printed instructions in the drill-book. Accustomed to formal battles fought in Flanders, they could not adjust themselves to the war against French Canadians and their Indian allies in the forests of the Ohio Valley and the shores of the Great Lakes.

Prince Leopold of Anhalt-Dessau, nicknamed 'the Old Dessauer', who had fought as Marlborough's ally at Blenheim, was primarily responsible for the reorganization of the Prussian army, which made

The opening pages of a drill book of 1745. Note that these eight drill movements do not include loading the weapon. The firing of a volley was still a tedious and lengthy business, not only for the man who had to perform the movements but for the officer who, in the din of battle, had to shout all the orders in the right sequence.

it the pattern for Europe in the eighteenth century. He gave to the infantry, all now armed with flintlock muskets and bayonets, an iron ramrod to replace the old wooden ones which often broke at a critical moment, leaving a man unarmed. This seemingly trivial change was in fact the most important technical advance in infantry equipment in the century. Prince Leopold also introduced a standard firearms drill which raised the rate of fire in Prussian units to as many as three shots a minute. This, in conjunction with a standard and equally meticulous foot-drill, turned a regiment or battalion into a manœuvrable machine producing a very considerable weight of fire on any front and in any direction or formation. The Prussian army was designed for attack based on swift tactical movements to exploit the slowness or mistakes of an enemy. Its precision and flexibility were unmatched in Europe. Naturally, many of Leopold's ideas were copied in France and England.

During the fourth decade of the century there were two major changes in the organization of the British army. The grenadier companies which hitherto had formed part of every Line regiment were grouped in grenadier battalions. They ceased to be true grenadiers and became specially selected shock troops. The second change was that for the first time since the Middle Ages, light troops, descendants

The Germans were the great exponents of military precision, uniformity and neatness. The Horse and the whipping post, in this Leipzig barracks of 1726, were constant reminders of the punishments awaiting any soldier lax in his dress or 'idle' in his drill exercises.

The grenadiers of three great Line Regiments in the middle of the eighteenth century.

of men like the Cornishmen who did so much damage with their long knives at Crécy, appeared in most continental armies. The need for them had evolved from the increasingly mechanical parade-ground tactics of infantry whose function was to produce volleys of musketry from close-packed formations. Something other than artillery was needed to harass, delay and perhaps break up these dense masses as they advanced across a battlefield with drums beating, in perfect step and alignment. The answer appeared to be small bodies of troops trained to scout and skirmish, to use ground and shoot accurately as individuals. These light companies, or 'flank companies' as they were called, were manned by picked soldiers who, because of the nature of their task, were the best in a battalion.

Although there were light troops at the Battle of Fontenoy in May 1745, the use of them was not really developed in the British army until the formation of the Royal American Regiment (later the 60th Foot and King's Royal Rifle Corps) in Pennsylvania in 1756.

The War of the Austrian Succession, another dynastic conflict, was the result of the death of the Emperor Charles VI of Austria in October 1740. His daughter, Maria Theresa, was the sole heiress to his dominions, and her right to succeed him had, before his death, been acknowledged by the European Powers in their Pragmatic Sanction. On his death this right was immediately challenged by three other candidates: Charles Albert, Elector of Bavaria, Philip V, King of Spain and Augustus III, King of Poland and Elector of

George II at the Battle of Dettingen, 1743. He was the last English monarch to lead his troops personally on active service.

Saxony. England took the side of Maria Theresa and Austria in an alliance with the Netherlands and Sardinia (Savoy) against France, Spain, Bavaria and Prussia. The two main battles fought by British troops in Europe were Dettingen in June 1743, and Fontenoy.

King George II, personally commanding the Allied army, marched from the Lower Rhine towards the River Main, hoping to drive a wedge between the French and Bavarians. His force of 37,000 British, Hannoverians and Hessians was trapped by the French Marshal, Duc Adrien Noailles, in a defile between Aschaffenburg and Hanau on the Main, but the French plan was upset by a premature charge by the French cavalry at the village of Dettingen. The King led his infantry in a fierce counter-attack and routed 28,000 Frenchmen before Noailles could react. This was the last battle in which a British monarch fought on the field.

At Fontenoy, two years later, William Augustus, Duke of Cumberland and son of George II, was in command. Fourteen thousand infantry in a compact wedge marched through murderous fire from two redoubts on their flanks straight into the centre of the French army led by the great Marshal Comte Maurice de Saxe. The enemy centre began to crumble, and this time it was the turn of the French to counter-attack furiously, against the flanks of the wedge. Losing more than 7,000 in dead and wounded, the British were forced to withdraw in good order, and during the night Cumberland retreated towards Brussels. Left on the field, the French claimed a victory.

Fontenoy was Britain's last battle in the war because her army had to be withdrawn from the Continent to deal with Prince Charles Edward's rising, which culminated in the defeat of the Young Pretender at Culloden on 16 April 1746. Cumberland's pursuit and ruthless slaughter of Jacobite rebels earned him the title of 'Butcher'.

In America, where ever since the founding of Quebec by Samuel Champlain in 1608 French settlers in Canada had been planning to contain the growth of English colonies on the Atlantic seaboard, the fighting was called 'King George's War'. In fact there had been intermittent fighting along the colonial borders for more than sixty years, but it had not flared into open warfare until King William's War in 1689. During their early struggles for existence the American Colonies received very little military aid from Britain. The first troops of the regular army to be stationed in America were drafts from the Grenadier and Coldstream Guards, formed into a battalion sent to deal with rebellion in Virginia in 1677.

There was no proper protection against such incidents as the French-inspired, and led, massacres by Indians at Casco, Salmon Falls and Schenectady in 1689. A certain number of training cadres

The Black Watch at Fontenoy, 1745. Painted long after the battle, the picture shows a wounded Ensign telling 'Butcher' Cumberland, who was to shed the blood of so many Highlanders at Culloden in the following year, to take note of those slain in England's cause.

of British officers crossed the Atlantic in 1706 to train the colonial militia, but the five regular battalions promised for an expedition against Montreal in 1709 never arrived because they were needed to replace the losses at Almanza. The first occasion on which a force from England played any part in the long struggle against the French in Canada was in June 1710. One regiment of marines and ships of the Royal Navy combined with a New England force to capture Port Royal (now Annapolis) in Acadia. In the following year a fleet commanded by Admiral Walker, carrying seven of Marlborough's best regiments to attack Quebec, ran into a storm off the Egg Islands in the mouth of the St Lawrence River. Eight ships were lost, 700 men were drowned and the whole project was abandoned. The French then built the great fortress of Louisbourg on Cape Breton Island which they used as a base for maritime and land operations, set up forts along the line of the Great Lakes and the Ohio Valley and began to encroach on the English Colonies.

Louis XV and George II formally declared war on each other in 1744. In the following year a force of raw New England militia led by a merchant, William Pepperrell, and assisted by three British warships under Commodore Warren, achieved what was deemed to be impossible, the capture of Louisbourg after a siege of six weeks. For the first time it became apparent to the military authorities in England that the American Colonist was a fighter in his own right, unorthodox, undisciplined but nevertheless dangerous. Yet the presence of British troops in North America, the fact that the Colonies were hopelessly disunited on practically every issue, and the obvious dependence of the Colonists on men and war material from Britain to protect them from the French, seemed to be adequate safeguards against trouble.

The great fortress of Louisbourg on Cape Breton Island, based on plans by Vauban. It was taken from the French by Pepperrell and his New Englanders, then handed back in exchange for Madras, and finally recaptured by Amherst and Wolfe.

In the West Indies, British units garrisoning Jamaica, the Bahamas, the Leeward Islands and Barbados wasted away, and battalions had to be replaced after only a year's service because of the diseases afflicting the men.

In India, from the time of the setting up of the first French trading 'factory' at Surat in 1668 – alongside the British one which had been there for more than fifty years – until the end of the War of the Spanish Succession in 1713, there were no hostilities between the English and French because neither were sufficiently well established to risk a conflict in the presence of strong native powers who were likely to throw them out if they created discord in the country. However, in 1720 a young Frenchman, Joseph François Dupleix, a man of formidable talents and energy and son of a Director of the French East India Company, arrived on the Coromandel Coast determined to build a great French colonial and commercial empire in the East, and at the same time drive out the British. For the next thirty-four years, until the French recalled Dupleix to Paris in disgrace in 1754, there was continuous warfare in southern India between European troops of the rival East India Companies, augmented by locally recruited sepoys. But the conflict in which Robert Clive, Colonel Stringer Lawrence, the Marquis de Bussy and the Comte de Lally played so prominent a part is not strictly part of the history of the British army. The first regular troops of the British establishment to serve in India were the 39th Foot (The Dorsetshire Regiment) and a small party of Royal Artillery taken out by Admiral Watson as reinforcements for Clive in the summer of 1754.

The Treaty of Aix-la-Chapelle was signed in 1748, and in Europe most of the conquered territory was restored to its former owners,

The Treaty of Aix-la-Chapelle, 1748. *A Representation of the several Potentates signing the Peace*, showing George II talking to the Queen of Hungary, Louis XV signing the 'Articles of Peace', and the King of Spain and Prince of Orange 'perusing them over'. In the background are various allegorical figures.

except for Silesia which passed to Prussia, then ruled by Frederick II (the Great). The rule of Maria Theresa was confirmed and her husband was recognized as the Holy Roman Emperor Francis I. One nail in the coffin of Anglo-American relations was the return to the French of Louisbourg, treasured Battle Honour of the New Englanders, in exchange for Madras.

The fighting in North America and India, and the depredations of privateers and raiding-parties in the Caribbean, continued, unaffected by European agreements. Despite this, the size of the armed forces at home was as usual drastically reduced. The strength of the British establishment was fixed at 30,000 men, two-thirds for home duties and one-third for garrisons overseas; and using all the familiar arguments against a standing army the politicians of both Houses made every effort to cut down the numbers even more. It was just as well that they were unsuccessful because within six years the army was heavily committed in the French and Indian War in North America, and two years later the Seven Years War broke out in Europe. Although it began as a recrudescence of the previous conflict – except that Prussia was now an enemy of France – the Seven Years War was a global struggle. William Pitt (later Lord Chatham) called it the first world war, and the British army fought in theatres as far apart as Canada and Bengal, north Germany and the Philippines.

In North America the arrival of a new French Governor of Canada, Duquesne, in 1752 marked the beginning of a determined effort by the French to restrict all British expansion towards the west. In the following year the twenty-one-year-old Adjutant of the Virginia militia, George Washington, led a small force to investigate the extent of the inroads being made on British colonial territory. He made plans for the building of a fort at the strategic point where the Monongahela and Allegheny rivers join to become the Ohio, but in April 1754 the workmen were driven off by a French expedition which took possession, rebuilt the strongpoint and named it Fort Duquesne.

Early in June 1755, the 44th and 48th Foot, in a mixed force which included thirty ratings from the Royal Navy, Virginia militia and Indian warriors, led by General Edward Braddock, set off to turn the French out of the Ohio Valley and establish garrisons to prevent their return. Braddock was ambushed in the forest near a ford of the Monongahela River, not far from Fort Duquesne, and because he would not break the rigid, Prussian-type infantry formation he had learned in Europe, his redcoats, massed in the open, were shot down by enemies they could not see. Braddock was mortally wounded. George Washington, who was one of his staff officers, was unscathed although his clothing was torn by several bullets. This defeat had far-reaching effects, for it was now apparent that stereotyped Prussian methods used against unorthodox and elusive enemies fighting in the 'wilderness of leaves' were suicidal. Other expeditions,

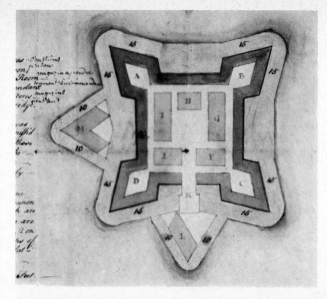

The Anglo-French war in North America gave the young George Washington invaluable experience, which he was later to use against the British in the War of American Independence. *Left:* Fort Duquesne, built by the French in 1754 after they had thwarted Washington's plans to construct a British stronghold on the same spot. *Below:* the ambushing in 1755 of General Braddock's force sent to drive the French from Fort Duquesne and the Ohio Valley. Washington, Braddock's staff officer, hurries forward as the General, shot through the lungs, falls from his horse.

against Fort Niagara and Crown Point, were equally unsuccessful, and not until July 1757 when Pitt took over all responsibility for running the war, did the tide of defeat begin slowly to turn. Even so, there were other disappointments before the influence of the 'Great Commoner' could be felt. The Duke of Cumberland was defeated at Hastenbeck in 1757, and only when the British troops in Europe came under the command of Ferdinand, Duke of Brunswick, did they establish their superiority on the battlefields of Germany. The Duke of Brunswick was Frederick the Great's outstanding general who, although always outnumbered, fought and won five consecutive campaigns.

At the end of 1757 General James Abercromby took over the command in America, and the plan for 1758 was that he would advance up the line of the Hudson and Richelieu rivers to take Montreal; General Jeffrey Amherst would take Louisbourg and move on to capture Quebec; and Brigadier-General John Forbes would wipe away the stain of Braddock's defeat by taking Fort Duquesne. Abercromby was fortunate in having Brigadier Lord

Major General James Wolfe

Howe as his second-in-command. Howe had studied forest warfare and he took infinite trouble to see that his men were properly trained and equipped for it. Instead of stockings and thin breeches the soldiers were given stout leggings to protect them from thorns; the long skirts of their coats were cut off; their gleaming musket-barrels and bayonets were browned, and unnecessary accoutrements in their knapsacks replaced by cornmeal to make them independent of supply columns. Finally their greasy queues were cut off and their powdered hair, no longer drawn back so tightly that a man could not close his eyes, was washed clean. Professional soldiers are conservative in their ways and some of his reforms were extremely unpopular, particularly among the Germans of the 60th Regiment who deeply resented the cropping of their long hair. But Howe turned an army of parade-ground dummies into a hard-marching field force of sharp-shooters.

It was a tragedy that Howe was killed in a little skirmish in the woods near Ticonderoga in July 1758, for the army's spirit and soul died with him. Abercromby, without Howe's sure hand to guide

A composite picture of Wolfe's attack on Quebec in 1759, showing the landing, the scaling of the Heights of Abraham and the battle on the plain outside the walls of the town. Both Wolfe (*below left*) and the French Commander-in-Chief, Montcalm, were mortally wounded.

him, launched his infantry in a series of unsupported frontal attacks against the Marquis de Montcalm's specially prepared position at Ticonderoga, and was utterly defeated. There was some compensation for this disaster in Amherst's success at Louisbourg and Forbes's expedition which took Fort Duquesne and renamed it Pittsburg.

Much had been happening in India, particularly in Bengal where the Nawab, Surajah Dowlah, alarmed by the growth of European influence in the Carnatic and determined to bring it under control in his own territories, had attacked and taken Calcutta in June 1756. His mistake was to confine 146 Europeans in a guard-house intended for 2 or 3 prisoners throughout one stifling June night, for there were only 24 survivors of the Black Hole of Calcutta. Clive took revenge at the Battle of Plassey, confronting Surajah Dowlah's army of 50,000 native troops and a contingent of French artillery with 900 Europeans (including the 39th Foot), 200 half-caste Portuguese and 2,100 sepoys. This victory brought the provinces of Bengal, Bihar and Orissa under British control at a cost of 23 of Clive's men killed and 49 wounded.

The year 1759 was the Year of Victories, and it began with the capture of the French settlements in West Africa, including the slaving station on the island of Goree, by Lieutenant-Colonel Worge, commanding the 76th Foot and two companies of the 66th. On the other side of the Atlantic Colonel Barrington captured Guadeloupe, richest of the French possessions in the Caribbean, in May. In Europe, on 1 August six regiments of British infantry (12th, 20th, 23rd, 25th, 37th and 51st) defeated the French under the Marshal Duc Louis de Contades in the remarkable Battle of Minden. 'I have seen what I never thought to be possible,' wrote Contades. 'A single line of infantry break through three lines of cavalry ranked in order of battle, and tumble them to ruin.' In India Colonel Forde took the French trading centre of Masulipatam and the province of the Northern Circars came into British hands. In North America, General Wolfe and his men scaled the Heights of Abraham in the dark hours before dawn on 13 September and defeated the Marquis de Montcalm in the subsequent battle on the plain outside the walls of Quebec. Both commanders died of wounds received in the battle. Meanwhile Amherst was advancing steadily up the line of the Hudson, the Lakes and the Richelieu River towards Montreal.

By the end of the year Britain had won her Empire; in the West Indies, in West Africa, in India and Canada. Her arms were triumphant in Europe and her navy supreme on all the oceans of the world. In January of the following year General Eyre Coote destroyed all effective French competition in India, for ever, by his defeat of the ill-fated Comte de Lally at the Battle of Wandiwash. And in the autumn Jeffrey Amherst completed the conquest of Canada by occupying Montreal.

General Sir Eyre Coote, victor of Wandiwash (1760), the battle which finally established the British as the supreme military power in India.

Chapter Three

THE DEFENCE OF EMPIRE

William Pitt's attitude to France throughout the Seven Years War had caused great alarm among the more timid politicians at Westminster. His aim had been the total destruction of French sea-power and the capture of all French overseas possessions, so that France would never again be able to seek revenge with sea-borne expeditions. It had very nearly been achieved, but Pitt's enemies argued that such a policy must set the whole world in arms against Britain. Unfortunately George II died suddenly in October 1760. His son, George III, was wont to listen more to Pitt's opponents than to his great minister, and in October 1761 Pitt resigned, having demanded in vain that war be declared on the Spanish King Charles III who had signed the (Bourbon) Family Compact with Louis XV. Thus Pitt had little say in the terms of the Peace of Paris (1763); even so, Britain received the whole of Canada, Nova Scotia and Cape Breton Island in North America, the whole of India except for the undefended towns of Pondicherry in the Carnatic and Chandernagore in Bengal, and in the West Indies the islands of Grenada, St Vincent, Tobago and Dominica; enormous increases to her Empire. But she handed back to France the islands of Guadeloupe, Martinique and St Lucia in the Caribbean, and Goree in West Africa. She also gave France fishing rights in the Gulf of St Lawrence, and Pitt claimed that all this 'restored France to her former greatness'. He foresaw that France would seize the first opportunity to be avenged for her losses and defeats.

William Pitt the Elder, subsequently Lord Chatham, the architect of victory in the Seven Years War which laid the firm foundations of the British Empire.

Meanwhile the land forces employed by Britain during the war, which had risen to a total of 203,000 men and had become a heavy burden to the taxpayers, were rapidly reduced, though not to levels as low as those after previous wars. In 1764 the peace establishment made provision for seventy infantry regiments, a reduction of thirty from the war strength. The allocation of manpower gave the home garrisons some 17,000 men; the Empire, 10,000; the Mediterranean bases of Gibraltar and Minorca, 4,000; and the Irish establishment, 12,000. The strength of the Royal Artillery was 1,800.

Despite all the battle experience of the past half-century, and all the experience of combined operations with the Royal Navy, there had been no real reform of British military organization. The responsibilities of Secretaries of State, the Secretary at War, the Master-General of the Ordnance, the Treasury and the Commander-in-Chief remained entirely unco-ordinated. More by accident than design the Commander-in-Chief, Lord Ligonier, a very capable man who was also Master-General of the Ordnance, became Pitt's military adviser and thus gained some degree of centralized control over the commanders of overseas theatres and home districts.

The army still had no transport system of its own and had to rely on 'impressment', the requisitioning of civilian resources, often by force, which did nothing to improve efficiency. There was no supply organization. Not until a war had actually begun were 'commissaries' appointed, and since they were civilians responsible to the Treasury, the local commander in the field had no control over them. Since there was no system, the maintenance of a force on active service depended very largely on the personal capabilities of the force commander – as it had in the days of Marlborough. Ligonier tried to straighten things out for the army in Germany by copying the Prussians and putting the commissariat on a military basis, under its own commander who was a member of Ferdinand of Brunswick's staff. Unfortunately the task was beyond the capacity of the officer selected.

Troops on the move. In the left foreground two bored soldiers of the baggage guard wait while the officers' possessions are loaded on requisitioned civilian transport.

Lord Jeffrey Amherst, conqueror of Canada: the great commander and administrative genius who was the equal of Marlborough and Wellington.

The lack of any properly organized supply system, and the principle of spreading responsibility among various government departments was one method by which Parliament ensured that power was not concentrated in the hands of the military.

Given this lack of system, Amherst's final campaign in Canada in 1760 was an astonishing achievement. His force moved on Montreal from three directions, he himself down the St Lawrence from Lake Ontario, Brigadier Haviland by way of Lake Champlain and the Richelieu River from the south, and Brigadier Murray up the St Lawrence from Quebec. Distances were vast and communications non-existent. All supplies had to be carried by canoe and humped over the portages. Two of the columns converged on the appointed day. Amherst himself, delayed by the need to reduce several enemy forts, was a few days late at the rendezvous. For administrative genius Amherst is the equal of Marlborough and Wellington, yet, because he gained all his military objectives by careful application of the age-old principles of war and without a major battle, he has never been given his rightful place in history.

The standard of recruits was seldom high, as this cartoon of the late eighteenth century makes clear.

The politicians' dislike of the army ensured that soldiers remained poorly treated and poorly paid. They had probably been induced to join up by unscrupulous recruiting sergeants who had filled them with drink and promises until they had become too befuddled and confused to resist. Once recruited, they were decked out in clothes that were too elaborate and too tight for comfort, hopelessly impractical for the tasks given to them. Believed to be incapable of thinking for themselves, they were told nothing of their immediate future or of their commander's intentions. Several contemporary French military writers comment on the fact that, without officers to lead them, British soldiers, even in the middle of a battle, appeared to be lost. This was apparent everywhere. Many sickened and died because they either neglected or were ignorant of the simplest precautions of personal hygiene. It is hardly surprising that at the slightest opportunity they drank themselves into oblivion.

William Pitt, Lord Chatham, had been right about the French need for revenge, and Louis XVI took immediate advantage of the situation which developed in the American Colonies.

The one strong link which for years had bound the Thirteen Colonies to the British Crown had been the need for military protection against the French in Canada. Had they been united in outlook and interests the Colonies might have been able to look after themselves, but each Colony regarded itself as independent and autonomous, and was so preoccupied with its own affairs that it was content to leave over-all defence to Britain. The expulsion of the French from North America removed both the threat and the last material bond with the mother country. Unaware of this, Britain, whose finances were now in the hands of the energetic George Grenville, tried to shift some of the huge burden of the French and Indian War on to the Colonies, and passed the unenforceable Stamp Act in 1765, thus providing the Colonists with an issue on which all could unite.

From the time of the so-called 'Boston Massacre' in March 1770, when six of the rabble were killed by soldiers they attacked outside

The Boston 'Massacre' of 1770, a good example of deliberate misrepresentation by the great American patriot Paul Revere. In a subsequent trial resulting from an investigation of the incident, the troops were ably defended by Bostonian attorneys.

Engrav'd Printed & Sold by PAUL REVERE BOSTON

Victory and defeat. *Above:* British troops enter New York in 1776 after Howe's successful campaign to take the city. *Opposite:* Lord Cornwallis surrenders at Yorktown in 1781. Washington, with the young Marquis de Lafayette on his right, towers over his contemporaries.

the Custom House, the New Englanders began to think seriously of war, yet right up to the time of firing the famous 'shot that echoed round the world' at Lexington on 19 April 1775 (though no one really knows who fired it) the British troops in America – derided as 'lobsters' and 'bloody-backs', a reference to the constant floggings – seem on the whole to have behaved with discipline and forbearance.

Few military authorities in England had any illusions about the war, even before it began. 'Taking America as it at present stands,' wrote Hervey, the Adjutant-General, 'it is impossible to conquer it with our British Army. To attempt to conquer it internally by our land force is as wild an idea as ever controverted common sense.' The general opinion in Britain was that operations should be entirely naval. If all American ports were occupied as naval bases, the external and coasting trade cut off completely and occasional destructive raids made on American stores and warehouses, the Colonies would soon adopt a more reasonable attitude. This might have been true, but British strategy was also founded on the entirely false assumption that the considerable number of known Loyalists would give active support to the regular troops in crushing the rebellion. The British government failed to appreciate that there is a great deal of difference between moral support and armed participation.

The war, in two phases and with varying degrees of intensity, went on for eight years. The first phase, which included the siege of Boston by the New Englanders, the Battle of Bunker (or more correctly Breed's) Hill, General Howe's capture of New York after the battles of Brooklyn, White Plains and Haarlem Heights, and George Washington's brilliant little success at Trenton, culminated in the surrender of 'Gentleman Johnny' Burgoyne's British force at Saratoga in October 1777. Hitherto France had supported the rebels clandestinely with money, war material and the sending of volunteers such as the young Marquis de Lafayette to give George Washington the benefit of up-to-date military advice. Saratoga was the turning-point of the war because it proved to the French that the 'united states' were capable of waging effective war. Louis XVI felt he had taken a great step towards the retribution he and his country sought for the defeats of the Seven Years War. He now came out into the open and signed commercial and political treaties with Benjamin Franklin in which France undertook to make war upon Britain until American independence was a reality.

The effect was not immediate. Far away to the south of Saratoga, Washington, trying to hold together the remnants of an army shattered by reverses at Brandywine Creek and Germantown, spent a dreadful winter at Valley Forge while the British, warm and dry in Philadelphia, lived well on the good beef and bread provided by

Americans who refused to give credit to the starving 'Patriots' in the field. Washington and his men survived the winter and by doing so kept the flag of rebellion flying. Thereafter the whole pattern of the war changed. In 1779 Spain joined France in the war against England. Holland followed suit in 1780, and in 1783 Britain was confronted by the League of Armed Neutrality which consisted of all the major and most of the minor states of Europe.

In July 1778 the French fleet from Toulon, commanded by the Comte d'Estaing, brought 4,000 French troops to aid the Colonists, and almost exactly a year later the Comte de Rochambeau landed with another French army at Rhode Island. The war in America became a series of battles between highly mobile forces, mainly in the south, and the end came when the British commander Lord Cornwallis set up his base at Yorktown in Chesapeake Bay. He was besieged by a combined American and French army under Washington and Rochambeau, and when a naval relieving force under the British Admiral Graves was defeated on 5 September 1781 by the French Admiral de Grasse and his fleet of forty men-of-war, Cornwallis surrendered – exactly four years to the day after Burgoyne's capitulation at Saratoga.

Britain and her army learned much from the War of American Independence, particularly on the relationship between sea-power and a colonial empire. It was not the army that lost America: commanders such as Gage, Howe, Clinton, Burgoyne and Cornwallis, and the troops they led, soon adapted themselves to a new kind of warfare in a vast theatre of operations where there was always a threat of unexpected action from local rebel militia. They abandoned the rigid formations deemed essential in Europe, fought in two ranks instead of three, in far more open order, and made use of cover. Special, highly mobile units of cavalry and mounted infantry were formed: the Legion, led by Major Banastre Tarleton, for example, and Simcoe's Rangers. The Legion had an unbroken record of success until defeated by Daniel Morgan in the classic little Battle of Cowpens; but in pitched battles such as Brandywine Creek, Germantown, Guildford Courthouse and Breed's Hill British troops won notable victories, indeed they won practically all their battles. The two surrenders at Saratoga and Yorktown were the result of flaws in over-all strategy combined with a complete lack of communications; they were not battlefield defeats. However, the main lesson of the war was that a handful of competent commanders and small bodies of troops, no matter how well trained, well disciplined and mobile, cannot conquer a continent.

Strangely enough the far-sighted Pitt had actively discounted what he called 'colonial disloyalty', but elsewhere his prophecy that England's enemies would avenge themselves for the Seven Years War was fulfilled. Britain lost Minorca, Gibraltar was long besieged but held out, and in the West Indies one island after another was taken by the French. It was in fact to avoid what might have developed into a national disaster that Britain acknowledged the independence of her American Colonies, and though the war went on for two years after the surrender at Yorktown it was brought to an end by the Treaty of Versailles in 1783.

When the British troops marched out of their camp at Yorktown to lay down their arms, their band appropriately enough played the tune 'The World Turned Upside Down', but no one could have foreseen the gigantic social upheaval that was coming. France was still in the grip of a monarchy both absolute and feudal, and her Three Estates of clergy, nobility and commons constituted a caste system apparently as immutable as anything devised in India, where Sir Eyre Coote was fighting and winning hard campaigns against the Mahrattas. Many of Rochambeau's troops deserted and became American citizens rather than return to France, and those who did go back took with them all sorts of strange ideas about life, liberty and the pursuit of happiness. Furthermore, France had ruined herself by intervening in America. Financial collapse, allied among other things with the spread of new ideas about social equality and the rights of man, led within six years to the French Revolution.

In England the nine years between the Treaty of Versailles and the outbreak in 1793 of the war to check the influence of the French Revolution were marked by rigid economy. The younger Pitt set out on a programme of financial reform which virtually ruined the army. For lack of recruits the Line regiments shrank to a handful of men, no Commander-in-Chief was appointed (to save money) and the Secretaries at War treated the post as a sinecure. The whole military system became rotten with chicanery and corruption. Promotion by purchase or favouritism placed rich dissolute young men and ignorant children in command of regiments. Drunkenness, absenteeism and all the worst abuses of the so-called 'military administration' of the eighteenth century rendered many regiments at home unfit for service of any kind, and the incompetence of the officers was rivalled only by the indiscipline of the men.

Yet there was at least one officer who took a professional interest in the army. In 1788, a booklet called *The Principles of Military Movement* was published by Colonel (later General Sir David) Dundas. He was convinced that the far more open formations and tactics developed during the American War would lead to disaster in the face of the massed volleys and close order of any continental enemy trained in the Prussian style. He advocated a return to the teachings of Frederick the Great. Since on the whole soldiers tend to think in terms of the last war and not the next one, his ideas were ridiculed. In the operations in the Carolinas, New Jersey and New York much had depended on the far more flexible tactics of light infantry, yet Dundas had hardly mentioned them. It had been forgotten that Wolfe, many years before, had written of the need for standard drill movements on the battlefield because of the tendency of lines of infantry to 'float' without them. Despite all the adverse criticism Dundas's book became an official drill-manual in the army, called *Rules and Regulations for the Movement of His Majesty's Army*, and it introduced into the infantry the 'steadiness' which was at the heart of all Wellington's victories.

For nearly four years after the fall of the Bastille in July 1789, Britain, with no intention of becoming involved in what was going on in France, kept her trade routes open and gained commercial advantages from the chaos across the Channel; but the seeds of revolutionary propaganda began to germinate. Disquieting symptoms of disloyalty became apparent in the regular army and the militia, a 'Jacobin Club' was founded in London and other revolutionary societies blossomed briefly. Pitt reacted sharply. Certain officers were dismissed – among them Lord Semphill of the 3rd Guards and Lord Edward Fitzgerald of the 54th Foot – and in December 1792 a large proportion of the militia was called out to act as a police force. This led the French to think that with a little encouragement a revolution similar to their own might be engineered in England.

In April 1792 France invaded the Austrian Netherlands, but the Revolution had had a marked effect on the great army created by the Duc de Choiseul and Louis XV; the Austrians in a small outpost opened fire and the leading French troops turned and ran. However, in September, when a force of Prussians, Austrians and French *émigrés* advanced towards Paris they were checked at Valmy by the veteran General Kellerman. For no known reason, Ferdinand, the Duke of Brunswick, the best general in Europe, commanding the invading army that was going to restore the monarchy in France, withdrew after a 'battle' that was no more than a cannonade. Valmy decided the fate of Europe.

The wars of the eighteenth century had been fought on a vast scale geographically, but their aims had been limited and in general participation had been confined to professional soldiers officered by the gentry. Objectives had been restricted and material, usually land or some commercial advantage. The armies of France in the Revolution, rallied by the slogan 'La Patrie en Danger!', went out to fight not a war but an ideological crusade. Their ranks were filled with citizens of every profession, trade and occupation, inspired, often enough, with blind idealism. From being an exercise mounted, operated and controlled by a small section of society, war became a national responsibility, and those countries of Europe which sought to contain the terrifying tide of revolution found that the mission of their military commanders was no longer the capture of a city or a province but the defence of their whole social system and way of life. Furthermore, the soldiers of France were not now the pressed and pipeclayed automatons in the white uniforms of Bourbon but men who were intelligent and educated and had minds of their own.

These citizen soldiers despised discipline because of its association with what they called the 'slaves of the despots' (the troops of other armies) and therefore the tactics of the Prussian school of military training were beyond their capabilities. They adopted instead a mass formation in which every man gained courage and enthusiasm from the proximity of his companions, and they discovered that these masses, or columns, hurtling headlong at the enemy's disciplined line, could punch their way through and cause the most gratifying havoc. Wearing far looser and more comfortable uniforms than the soldiers of the *ancien régime*, the new armies of France marched at great speed, fought in battalion columns which advanced behind a cloud of skirmishers and attacked wherever their artillery had had the most effect. If they did form a line it was always supported by columns. Their tactics could well be summed up in the words of Danton the revolutionary: 'De l'audace, encore de l'audace, et toujours de l'audace.' The French army was perhaps more formidable now than it had ever been. Its artillery was of the highest standard, it possessed a hard core of old professional soldiers, behind it lay generations of military tradition, it was motivated by great ideals of liberty, equality and brotherhood, and it was supported by most of the nation as a national institution.

Soldiers of the French Revolutionary Army (in its early stages) being addressed by the equivalent of a political commissar, a 'representative' of the Convention. (Note the bare-footed wounded man on the extreme left.)

Britain had no wish to face this new French army at a time when her own was in such a sorry state. But she was being forced into war by her concern for the navigational artery of the Scheldt, whose security she had guaranteed to Holland, and by the rejection of a series of diplomatic Notes, sent to the French Convention, which stated her determination not to allow France to acquire Belgium or invade Holland. The execution of Louis XVI on 21 January 1793 so distressed Pitt and his ministers that he ordered Chauvelin, the French Ambassador, to leave the country. This upset the Convention in Paris, and on 1 February France declared war on Britain and Holland. Thus began the war which, except for two brief pauses, was to end in the muddy rye-fields on the slopes of Mont St Jean at Waterloo.

The opening campaign in Flanders, conducted by Frederick, Duke of York, was disastrous, but the Duke himself learned a great deal from it. He has been much condemned as a military commander but it is unlikely that anyone else who was faced with his problems would even have done as well as he did. His allies were quarrelsome and unco-operative, he had no administrative services and no support from the politicians at home. His army consisted of officers who in general knew nothing of their so-called 'profession', and soldiers whose chief characteristic was habitual drunken-

An unfair cartoon by Gillray showing how the Duke of York conducted the campaign in Flanders. He and his staff feast on food and drink brought to them by soldiers who are mere skeletons.

FATIGUES OF THE CAMPAIGN IN FLANDERS.

The LONGITUDE and LATITUDE
of Warley Camp in the Summer of 1795

Another cartoonist's opinion of the officers who were to protect England from invasion by the French.

ness. It was impossible for a young officer to live on his pay, received spasmodically and months in arrears. Most of them were burdened by debts incurred under the purchase system, and though prize-money and loot sometimes enabled them to buy food and replace clothing and shoes worn out on campaigns, if the fortunes of war went against them many, particularly the subalterns, literally starved.

Conditions were bad enough for the officers but they were dreadful for the men. Most of their nominal pay was deducted for food and necessaries they seldom received and thousands died from cold and exposure, disease and starvation in the Flanders campaign as they marched barefoot through the mud.

In 1795 the Duke of York was made Field-Marshal on the Staff, an appointment which became that of Commander-in-Chief, and as such he was responsible for a certain amount of artillery and a number of cavalry and infantry regiments which, for the most part, appeared to be lacking in loyalty, discipline, organization and administration, and contained officers and men of the worst type. Within seven years he created from this unpromising material an army which not only defeated the 'unconquerable' veterans of France, Napoleon's 'old moustaches', but became a political influence of great value to Britain in the councils of Europe.

From the Letter Books and records of the period it is clear that the Duke had an unusual capacity for work and attention to detail.

Though not a great commander in the field he was unquestionably a great administrator who was really concerned about the efficiency and well-being of the ordinary soldier, and he insisted that officers should look after as well as lead their men. By demanding a proper acceptance of responsibility he restored to a certain extent the sense of brotherhood so strong in Britain's field armies of the Middle Ages, and since he required fixed standards of professionalism, men were able to respect their officers. He put an end to the commissioning of infants, and though he could not abolish the purchase system altogether he laid down a time-scale. For example, no one could purchase the rank of major until he had served six years as an officer, and the lowest age for a cornet of cavalry or ensign of infantry was set at sixteen. He introduced periodical confidential reports on officers and maintained a list of those who were able but impecunious, whom he promoted on merit and without purchase. He also lent his prestige and support to the founding of the Royal Military College in 1802, which had a Junior Department (later the Royal Military College, Sandhurst) to train young men as junior officers, and a Senior Department (later the Staff College, Camberley) to train older officers for the staff. Hitherto, military schools had been intended only for the sons of serving officers; for example, the Royal Military Academy at Woolwich for the sons of artillery officers, and Addiscombe in Kent for the sons of officers of the Army of the Honourable East India Company. In 1803 the Duke also founded the Depot of Military Knowledge, on the top floor of Horse Guards, which was the origin of the military intelligence organization and the Survey Department.

Frederick, Duke of York, completed the work of the Duke of Cumberland who, in 1748, had been so distressed by the administrative chaos in the army, revealed during the War of the Austrian Succession, that he had done his best to organize a staff structure and lay down channels of communication which put an end to the Secretary of War's habit of dealing direct with junior officers.

Recruiting, discipline and the internal administration of regiments, clothing, equipment, training and the movement of troops were all controlled by specific regulations and made the responsibility of the Adjutant-General and the Quartermaster-General. A new post, that of Military Secretary, was created in 1793, dealing with all aspects of officers' promotion and postings. With so much of the army's administration now in the hands of professional officers the importance of the political Secretary at War began to decline.

In France, conscription which brought 'respectable citizens' into the army, and the guillotine which removed a large number of officers of the old aristocracy, combined to close the gap between officer and soldier and to create an informal relationship. In England, where conscription was never considered, this could not happen yet, largely because there was still no real incentive to join the army. The ranks contained mostly either penniless Catholic Irishmen

Frederick, Duke of York, the man who, from the most unpromising material, fashioned the army that defeated Napoleon's veterans.

whose splendid fighting qualities were overbalanced by their ill discipline, violence, and passion for drink, or criminals of one sort or another from the gaols. The number of intelligent and respectable men of the Sergeant Lamb, Edward Costello and Private Wheeler type, who wrote lucid and fascinating accounts of their adventures, was very small indeed.

Just before the war with France began in 1793 the pay of a private soldier was raised from William III's rate of eightpence a day to one shilling. Though issued with bread, a man had to buy all his other food and cleaning materials, and the deductions and stoppages from his gross pay left him with only about eighteen shillings a year – at a time, moreover, of soaring inflation. Naturally enough, soldiering could not compare with any other occupation which provided a daily or weekly wage. Soldiers were always hungry and driven to steal food to keep alive.

Discipline was maintained principally by the lash, the cat-o'-nine-tails whose leather 'tails' were usually knotted, sometimes round small pieces of lead, and always tore the victim's back to

A man is flogged 'at the halberds'. The punishment, administered by a drummer, is supervised by the Drum Major, the regimental doctor and an officer of the regiment.

shreds. Sentences of 1,000 lashes were not uncommon and there are many contemporary descriptions of the administration and effects of a flogging. Much has been written of this brutality, and though repellent by modern standards, it must be judged in the context of an age of violence in which children convicted of petty theft were hanged. Not only the generals – even the more enlightened such as Sir John Moore and Wellington – believed flogging was essential if the army was not to degenerate into a mob of criminals, and the better elements of the rank and file looked upon it as a form of protection. Without it, as Quartermaster-Sergeant Anton of the 42nd Highlanders wrote, 'the good must be left to the mercy of the worthless'. Difficult though it is to put anything so controversial in its right perspective, the author of *A Soldier In Time of War*, John Stevenson, a man with twenty-one years' service in the Guards, no doubt expressed the opinion of many when he wrote: 'They talk of the lash. I was never any more afraid of the lash than I was of the gibbet, no man ever comes to that but through his own conduct.' On the retreat to Corunna in 1808–9 Sir John Moore appealed entirely without success to the better nature of his troops. 'Black Bob' Craufurd, famous commander of the Light Division on the same fearful march, had other ideas and his own way of dealing with men who left the ranks. Two men fell out on one occasion, and one of his soldiers wrote: 'No one but one formed of stuff like General Craufurd could have saved the Brigade from perishing altogether; and if he flogged two, he saved hundreds from death.'

The Duke of York turned his army into a splendid fighting force. For the first time cavalrymen were trained in the use of the sword. Putting into effect what was laid down in the manual written by Colonel Le Marchant (original founder of the Staff College) called *The Rules and Regulations for the Attainment and Practice of the Sword*

The reorganization and
retraining of the army under
the Duke of York. *Left:
Cut two against Infantry*; a
new discipline was instilled
into the cavalry with the help
of Le Marchant's manual on
swordsmanship, from which
this illustration is taken.
Below: an officer of
the 7th Light Dragoons,
armed with the
huge, unwieldy cavalry
sabre. *Below left:* a
rifleman and an officer of the
95th Foot, formed out of the
Corps of Riflemen and later
to become the Rifle Brigade.

Exercise, the horsemen ceased to chop their own toes and slash the ears off their own horses and chopped and slashed the enemy instead. Yet even with this new discipline, cavalrymen, by tradition brave to the point of stupidity, were a trial to Wellington who complained that they *would* gallop everywhere and 'could not preserve their order'.

In 1797 the Duke of York began to reorganize the light companies of the infantry, and he issued special instructions for training them, particularly in musketry. In the summer manœuvres of the following year he collected together an experimental formation of light infantry, light Horse and Horse Artillery (first introduced by Prince Rupert of the Rhine in 1642 during the Civil War). This was the embryo of the Light Division in the Peninsular War. When serious threats of a French invasion in 1803 brought large concentrations of troops into south-eastern England, the Duke gave to Sir John Moore the task of training light troops at Shorncliffe Camp on the basis of a book written by a German officer, Major-General Baron de Rothenburg, called *Regulations for the Exercise of Riflemen and Light Infantry*. In 1800, again on the instructions of the Duke of York, a Corps of Riflemen was formed, and it consisted of detachments, sent by each regiment for training, which were to return to their units afterwards. While these detachments were all together in Windsor Forest they were sent off on a combined operation to raid Ferrol. They stayed together as the 95th Foot, expanded into three battalions and in 1816 were given the name of the Rifle Brigade.

Although German and Austrian light troops had possessed rifled small-arms forty years before, in the Seven Years War, as had the Royal American Regiment, their weapons had all been hunting-rifles, made individually by craftsmen, which were not suitable for mass production. Any muzzle-loading rifle was more accurate than the smooth-bore musket and had a greater range. Much of the muzzle velocity of a musket was lost by 'windage', the explosive force of the charge escaping round the ill-fitting shot as it went up the barrel. But the rate of fire of a rifle was slower because the bullet had to be rammed down the rifling. However, in 1800, as the result of tests by the Ordnance Board, the British Baker rifle was selected for riflemen of the light companies and the 95th Regiment; furthermore, for the first time a concession was made towards camouflaging forward troops when the 95th were given green uniforms – the forerunners of khaki. Prussian and Austrian light troops had been wearing 'gamekeeper' green for years; it was Napoleon's favourite colour.

Tactics remained virtually unaltered. Dundas's advice on standardized close-formation drill was acknowledged to be valuable when troops had to face the shock tactics of the French columns, and the skirmishing riflemen could begin their harassing of the enemy at greater ranges. The decisive factors on the battlefield were still reckoned to be the point-blank volleys of massed infantry and the impact of cavalry. The bayonet was rather more frightening than lethal, because the threat of a bayonet charge was usually enough; few troops would stand and close with ranks of men determined to use it.

Though subsequently found entirely innocent of accusations made against him personally, the Duke of York resigned as Commander-in-Chief in 1809 when the scandal concerning the attempted trafficking of his mistress, Mary Anne Clarke, in commissions and promotions came to light. She had obtained large sums from various people on the assurance that she could persuade the Duke to commission or promote them. In fact she was never successful and they lost their money. Fortunately the Duke's invaluable reforms were almost complete; but he had not had time to co-ordinate the higher echelons of command, so that all the separate departments could be united in purpose and directed along a single strategic path to a common aim.

Pitt's attempts to unite Europe in the First Coalition, to conquer France and end the French Revolution, came to an ignominious end in April 1795 when, through no real fault of his own, the Duke of York was compelled to withdraw the British army from the Continent. By 1797 Britain's only ally was Portugal. France had occupied Belgium, Holland, the Rhineland and northern Italy. In three years the armies of the French Republic had achieved all that the *ancien régime* had tried for two centuries to obtain. This success was largely the result of Britain's failure to send an effective force across the Channel in the early stages, and there was little she could do now except hang on, apply the old maritime policy of the Tories, and mount combined operations against the new French empire

Gillray's view of the militia.

Anon Bond Street.
S.ʳ GEORGE'S-VOLUNTEERS Charging the FRENCH, after clearing the Ring in Hyde Park, & Storming the Dunghill at Marybone.

71

British troops moving
forward to attack enemy
positions in the Helder
campaign – a combined
operation – of 1799.

in Europe and overseas wherever there seemed to be any hope of
success. Pitt was confident that a war of attrition, centred on the
capture of the West Indian islands which were the sources of much
of France's wealth, would bring victory in the long run. This was
the opinion of an economist, not a strategist.

Meanwhile France began to make preparations for her own 'maritime policy', an invasion of the British Isles. Ireland was the vul-
nerable flank. Irishmen who longed for complete independence
were promised armed assistance from France to realize their dream,
and they began to muster their forces. In 1797 a motley force
calling itself the 'Black Legion', led by an American adventurer,
Colonel Tate, sailed from Brest to wreak havoc on the west coast
of England. Landing on 22 February near the lonely village of
Fishguard, this 'French invasion' was rounded up by the local
militia before any damage was done.

In the following year, anticipating help from France, Ireland
exploded into full-scale rebellion, but General Lake and a small
force of regular troops destroyed the rebel cause at the Battle of
Vinegar Hill before the French arrived. The rebellion was over by
the time General Humbert and 900 French troops landed at Killala
Bay in County Mayo, and though they repulsed Lake at Castlebar,
they were surrounded and forced to surrender at Ballinamuck a
fortnight later.

In 1798 Napoleon set out to conquer India from the base he proposed to establish in Egypt. Nelson bore down on the French fleet as it lay at anchor in Aboukir Bay. 'Victory', he said next morning, as the smoke of burning French warships swirled in thick clouds across the beach, 'is not a name strong enough for such a scene.' Napoleon and his army were stranded in Egypt and news of the Battle of the Nile revived the European Coalition. Another British expedition to the Continent, the campaign of the Helder in the summer of 1799, was no more successful than the first. General Brune, regarded by Napoleon as one of the least competent of his commanders, conducted a spirited defence among the fever-ridden waterways and drove the British out of Holland.

Napoleon abandoned his army in Egypt, returned secretly to France and shattered the Austrian Army of Italy at Marengo in June 1800. Marshal Nicolas Soult threw the Russian Marshal Count Aleksandr Suvorov out of Switzerland, and Moreau defeated the Austrian army in Germany at Hohenlinden. The Second Coalition ceased to exist. General Junot marched into Spain, on into Portugal and occupied Lisbon, thus depriving Britain of her only access to Europe. The capture of Minorca and Malta from the French was meagre compensation.

Pitt and Henry Dundas, responsible for direction of the war, did not appreciate the real value of sea-power, and instead of using it to land a balanced concentration of force where it was least expected and likely to achieve the best results, they wasted their resources on tip-and-run raids, such as the pointless expeditions to Cadiz and Ferrol. It was their failure to support the Second Coalition that led to its dissolution. The first proper use of their command of the sea was the landing of General Sir Ralph Abercrombie's army over the beach at Aboukir on 8 March 1801, against the marooned but well-entrenched force left behind by Napoleon. Victory, the first by the army created by Frederick, Duke of York, was complete. Cairo was taken, all the French were rounded up, and Egypt was handed back to the Ottoman Empire.

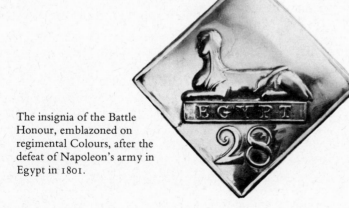

The insignia of the Battle Honour, emblazoned on regimental Colours, after the defeat of Napoleon's army in Egypt in 1801.

The storming of
Seringapatam in India in
1799. The body of the Sultan
of Mysore, Tippoo Sahib,
was found in a huge mound
of enemy corpses under the
northern gateway.

In India, where Marquis Wellesley was Governor-General, the agents of the French Republic had been active among the native potentates. But the Marquis's younger brother, the twenty-nine-year-old Colonel Arthur Wellesley, fought a series of brilliant campaigns, first against the Sultan of Mysore, Tippoo Sahib (who was to have been Napoleon's ally in destroying the British) and then against the Mahrattas. Tippoo Sahib was killed when his capital at Seringapatam was taken. Mysore and Hyderabad became puppet states. 'The British came here in the morning,' wrote one of the Mahratta leaders, 'looked over the wall, walked over it, killed all the garrison and retired for breakfast.'

In the set-piece Battle of Assaye in 1803, Arthur Wellesley, promoted to Major-General, smashed the well-organized and highly efficient Mahratta army of 40,000 men, a feat equal to if not surpassing Clive's victory at Plassey. Britain became the undisputed military power in India.

In 1802 Pitt's government fell over the question of Irish Catholic emancipation from the penal statutes imposed by William III after the Battle of the Boyne. His successor, Addington, anxious to end the war, signed the Treaty of Amiens. It brought only a brief pause in hostilities.

Chapter Four

VICTORY, STAGNATION
AND REFORM

On 18 May 1803, Pitt, now back in power, declared war on France. He had come, accurately enough, to the conclusion that Napoleon had signed the Treaty of Amiens simply to gain time and freedom from the pressures of war to make his plans for the invasion of Britain. In March 1803 Napoleon had ordered a vast but impracticable programme of boat-building. He needed 2,000 small craft to convey 120,000 men across the Channel in the first wave of the invasion. In June he detached from his national army of half a million men a force of 200,000 which he called the 'Army of the Coasts of the Ocean'. Divided into separate army corps these troops concentrated in coastal areas from Ostend to St Malo. Ironically, the respectable citizens of England, who so despised the army, put on the uniforms of fencibles, volunteers and militia to support the regular army in the defence of the country against the all-conquering French veterans. Fortunately – if the cartoonist Gillray's opinion of the volunteer forces was justified – this amateur army was not required to prove its worth. The Royal Navy maintained its command of the narrow seas.

A sudden resurgence of Austrian militarism put an end to Napoleon's invasion plans and by 1 September 1805 the Army of the Coasts of the Ocean was marching south across Europe towards Ulm to prevent one of the Austrian armies from joining its Russian allies. Thus, although Nelson's victory at Trafalgar ended all the invasion scares in England, the attack on England had already been called off and the naval battle had no significant effect on the campaigns of the Third Coalition. After his victory at Ulm Napoleon occupied Vienna and on 2 December 1805, 87,500 Russians and Austrians were utterly defeated by 73,000 Frenchmen at Austerlitz. This 'Battle of the Three Emperors' wrecked the Third Coalition. In the following year Prussia, whose military machine had been so magnificent under Frederick the Great and Ferdinand of Brunswick but was now a parade-ground army led by old men, was unwise

enough to declare war on France. Pitt died in 1806 and so did not
see the shattering defeats of the Prussian army at Jena and Auerstadt.
Napoleon then moved against Russia, and after victories at Eylau in
February and Friedland in June 1807 imposed on the Tsar at Tilsit
a treaty as humiliating as the one he had made the Austrians sign at
Pressburg. He was now master of all Europe except Great Britain
and the Iberian peninsula; for although Junot was in Lisbon,
Charles IV still sat on the Spanish throne.

Learning that under a secret clause in the Treaty of Tilsit Napoleon
was to acquire the Danish navy and control of the entrance to the
Baltic, in August 1807 the British government sent a fleet under
Admiral Gambier, carrying a land force in which General Sir Arthur
Wellesley again distinguished himself, on a successful expedition to
seize the Danish fleet.

The war appeared to have reached the condition of stalemate.
Napoleon lacked the naval resources for invasion, and Britain,
without enough soldiers and no effective allies left on the Continent,
could not attempt an invasion herself.

In 1808 Napoleon lured the Spanish King Charles IV and his son
Ferdinand to Bayonne, and under the threat of a firing-squad –
loading its muskets ostentatiously in the yard outside the window –
forced the King to abdicate. He then appointed his own brother
Joseph 'to the crowns of Spain and of the Indies'. A lone Spanish
horseman carried the news to Madrid and on 2 May, the famous

Napoleon as First Consul
(*above*) in 1803, and as
Emperor (*opposite*) in 1807
signing the Treaty of Tilsit
with Alexander on a raft in
the River Niemen.

Dos de Mayo, the Spanish nation rose in revolt against the Corsican usurper. Joachim Murat, that flamboyant French marshal and cavalryman, quelled the rising in Madrid in exactly four hours. One hundred 'revolutionaries' were shot – Goya has depicted the scene with searing accuracy – and the rest were told to go home. Spain appealed to England for help. In August Sir Arthur Wellesley, whom Napoleon contemptuously described as 'the sepoy general', landed with an army of 30,000 men at the mouth of the River Mondego and defeated the French under General Junot first at Roliça and then Vimiero. Had Wellesley not been superseded in command by the elderly and incompetent Sir Harry Burrard and Sir Hew Dalrymple, Junot's force would have been pursued and annihilated. As it was, the Convention of Cintra was signed and the French were sent back to France – in British warships. All three generals were ordered to return home and Sir John Moore took over command of an army of 40,000. Britain, the naval power, at last had her foothold on the Continent.

Moore was told to advance to Madrid, co-ordinate his operations with the Spanish army – whose General Castanes had already brought about the surrender of General Dupont and 22,000 Frenchmen at Baylen – and throw the French out of Spain. The French disaster at Baylen had been the first small crack in the huge imperial edifice. To repair it, Napoleon himself crossed the Pyrenees with 250,000 men, Horse, Foot and Guns, and this tide of steel swept through Spain to replace 'King' Joseph on the throne he had left very hurriedly after Dupont's capitulation. One of Moore's intelligence officers, Captain John Waters, intercepted a message

Napoleon's brother Joseph, the timid and entirely unsuccessful 'King of Spain and of the Indies'.

Sir John Moore and his troops crossing the Tagus near Villa Velha.

Opposite: Arthur Wellesley, First Duke of Wellington, in the Peninsula – wearing the famous blue coat in which he fought most of his Spanish campaigns.

from the French Chief of Staff, Berthier, to Marshal Soult, and Moore, warned of the trap awaiting him, swung north-west from Salamanca and raced for the sea. A blizzard, howling through the passes of the Sierra de Guadarrama, delayed the French pursuit. Napoleon handed over to Soult and returned to Paris. Moore, after an appalling march, reached Corunna in January 1808 to find that the fleet he expected was not in the harbour. He turned, and with his back to the sea, fought off Soult's determined efforts to destroy him. Moore was killed in the battle but his army was saved and subsequently evacuated.

The British, except for their small garrison in Lisbon, had been thrown out of the Peninsula, but Wellesley, restored to high command, returned three months later, drove Soult out of Oporto and with an army of 20,000 British and an equal number of Spanish under General Cuesta, marched into Spain. On 28 July 1809 he met Marshal Victor in a set-piece battle at Talavera. The Spanish, unequalled as guerrilla fighters, proved to be alarmingly unreliable, and 16,000 British had to face the assaulting columns of more than 30,000 French. Victor lost 7,300 men and 20 guns in a fierce battle and limped back to Madrid. Nevertheless, Wellesley had suffered more than 5,000 casualties and had to withdraw down the Tagus into Portugal. His reward for his victory was elevation to the peerage as Viscount Wellington.

These British victories, at Roliça, Vimiero and Talavera, were an unpleasant shock to the 'invincible' French. Throughout Europe, and although often outnumbered, their tactics of the cannonade followed by the tremendous impact of the column had accustomed them to victory. They had learned to despise British troops. The

British efforts in Flanders and Holland, and at Ostend in 1798, had been contemptible; even old Brune had been able to defeat them. But Talavera in particular was an unpleasant surprise. The British cavalry charged with a most disconcerting determination; the rate of fire of the artillery, and its accuracy, were as good as that of the French, and the infantry, standing in its thin red lines, was unnervingly steady.

Strangely enough the answer to the tactics of the French had been revealed to several British commanders in an obscure little battle fought on the dusty plain of Maida, on the instep of Italy, between 5,000 British and 6,000 Frenchmen on a scorchingly hot July day in 1806. The battle had been the result of one of many nuisance raids on the coast of Napoleon's empire, and though of virtually no strategic significance it was, tactically, a turning-point of the war. The French columns had attacked four separate British brigades, each brigade being drawn up in two ranks, commanded by Brigadier-Generals Cole, Kempt, Oswald and Acland (the old concept of the long unbroken line had been made obsolete by the campaigns in North America against the unorthodox tactics of the rebel forces). The French lost 2,000 men. British casualties were 300. It had proved to be a simple matter of fire power and mathematics. In a French column of 800 men, 60 men wide, only the first two ranks (120 men) could fire at the enemy while on the move. The rest of the column merely surged along behind, shouting warlike cries. In the British force, with the rear rank covering off the gaps between the men in the front rank, every soldier could use his musket. Volleys, fired in turn by the whole front rank and the whole rear rank at close range, tore into the front and flanks of the advancing column, checking, halting and finally blasting them to pieces. The French had not previously encountered an enemy who stood absolutely steady to meet the impact of the running column, and it had not occurred to them that they could be stopped merely by musketry. The brigadiers at Maida passed on the tactical lessons they had learned, and all of them fought under Wellington in the Peninsula.

Several French generals, including General Foy, have left descriptions of what it was like to be in an attacking column against Wellington's troops; one of the best was written by Marshal Bugeaud:

[As the column moved forward] some men hoisted their shakos on their musket, the quick-step became a run; the ranks began to be mixed up; the men's agitation became tumultuous, many soldiers began to fire as they ran. And all the while the red English line, still silent and motionless, even when we were only 300 yards away, seemed to take no notice of the storm which was about to break on it. . . . At this moment of painful expectation the English line would make a quarter-turn – the muskets were going up to the 'ready'. An indefinable sensation nailed to the spot many of our men, who halted and began to open a wavering fire. The enemy's return, a volley of simultaneous

precision and deadly effect, crashed upon us like a thunderbolt. Decimated by it we reeled together.... Then three formidable *Hurrahs!* terminated the long silence of our adversaries. With the third they were down upon us, pressing us into disorderly retreat....

To imply that all Wellington's victories were defensive battles and the result of opposing the French column with the British line is to ignore all the complications introduced by cavalry, artillery, skirmishers and the actual ground on which the battles were fought. Essentially, however, his victories were based on two principles: one was the choosing of ground which afforded some protection from the preliminary cannonade, and from cavalry – very often a reverse slope position – and the other was fire-power, the concentration of every available weapon on the target. The extremely unnerving British habit of remaining quite silent and quite still until all the muskets moved together and the bright bayonets flashed once in the sunlight was in the best tradition of the archers who stood motionless in the open along the ridge between Crécy and Wadicourt, waiting for the French to come within range.

By continental standards the British force in the Peninsula was always small, little more than what the French regarded as an army corps, but, as Canning had said of Moore's expedition in 1808, 'it is not merely a considerable part of the dispensable force of this country. It is, in fact, the British Army.'

Lady Butler's famous picture of the Diehards at Albuhera in 1811, *Steady the Drums and Fifes.*

Wellington fought his battles with this fact very much in mind. 'Since this is the only army Britain has,' he said, just before the Battle of Fuentes d'Onoro, 'we must look after it.' Wellington, like Marlborough before him, by his own talents and the force of his dominating personality, welded his army into an efficient, co-ordinated force. Only a man with his energy and powers of command could have succeeded in overcoming all the disadvantages inherent in a system in which his staff and his services owed their allegiance to departments of the War Office and not to him personally as the commander. By 1814 his Quartermaster-General, Sir George Murray, had become the equivalent of a Chief of Staff, and his army was organized on the divisional basis with attached supporting artillery and signals, medical and intelligence services. His staff knew their functions and the *esprit de corps* of his units was higher than ever before.

The great Battle of Albuhera, fought on 16 May 1811, in which the British under Marshal Beresford refused to be defeated by Soult, was won by pure *esprit de corps*. 'There is no beating these troops, in spite of their generals,' wrote Soult after the battle. 'I always thought they were bad soldiers; now I am sure of it. I had turned their right, pierced their centre and everywhere victory was mine, but they did not know how to run.' Colonel Inglis, badly wounded by grapeshot, lay in front of his men exhorting them, 'Die hard, 57th! Die hard!'

Lady Butler's picture, *Steady the Drums and Fifes*, her tribute to the Diehards, must be one of the best-known military paintings. Such was the spirit in the Peninsular Army that no unit would consider leaving the field while any other Regiment of the Line remained upon it.

The war in the Peninsula lasted for six years, but the turning-point
came in March 1811 when the veteran Marshal Massena was forced

Yet the men, because of their background and character, still posed special problems. In 1812 a civilian, Mr Judge Advocate Larpent, went out to Spain to put army discipline on a proper footing and be Wellington's legal adviser. Wellington was constantly infuriated by the behaviour of troops to the local Portuguese and Spanish inhabitants, not because he had any particular love for the Iberians but because they were his main source of intelligence.

The war in the Peninsula lasted for six years, but the turning-point came in March 1811 when the veteran Marshal Massena was forced to retreat from the impregnable lines of Torres Vedras. In 1812 Wellington moved over to the offensive, beat Marshal Marmont and his army of 40,000 men in forty minutes at Salamanca, occupied Madrid and laid siege to Burgos. Badly let down by his engineers and not having enough siege artillery he was compelled to go all the way back to Portugal, but in 1813 he advanced again, completely routed the French at Vittoria, fought his way through the Pyrenees and in 1814 ended his great campaign in triumph with the capture of Toulouse.

The Battle of Toulouse began at 2 a.m. on 10 April 1814 and ended at 4 p.m. Soult withdrew to Villefranque, Wellington entered Toulouse in triumph and the Peninsular War was over.

Meanwhile the indestructible Austrians had once more taken the field (in 1809) only to be forced yet again into a crippling peace after the Battle of Wagram in July of that year. There is no doubt that the unfortunate Austrians, never able to defeat Napoleon – except partially at Aspern, two months before Wagram – yet so often faced by the main weight of the French army, contributed materially to the downfall of Napoleon by inflicting so many casualties in his armies.

Of the 500,000 men who followed Napoleon to Moscow in 1812 only 20,000 returned, and the power of France began to wane. Prussia came back into the war in 1813 and, with her Russian allies, was again beaten at Lützen and Bautzen. Austria, revived by the news of Vittoria, tried once more, and this time the forces of Austria, Prussia and Russia inflicted a crushing defeat on Napoleon. After this great 'Battle of the Nations' at Leipzig the French Emperor, one of the most aggressive commanders in military history, fought a brilliant defensive campaign as he tried unsuccessfully to stem the Allies' advance upon Paris. His exile in Elba followed.

His escape in 1815 led to three more battles, in Flanders, where the war of 1793 had begun. The Prussians were defeated at Ligny and the British had to fall back after the confused encounter battle at

Cruikshank's cartoon of Napoleon, defeated at the 'Battle of the Nations' in 1814, being dragged off to captivity in Elba by one of the Cossacks he had failed to destroy in the disastrous Russian campaign of 1812.

Quatre Bras. Then Napoleon and Wellington fought the last battle of their military careers at Waterloo.

The Battle of Waterloo, 1815: a British gun crew in action.

Wellington had almost no veterans. Most of his great Peninsular regiments were either campaigning in America – where they burned the White House in the partially built town of Washington – or in garrisons overseas. Of his army of 67,000 men in Flanders, only 24,000 were British, and they were inexperienced. The rest were German – Hannoverians, Brunswickers and the King's German Legion – and Dutch and Belgians, all of doubtful quality. Napoleon's army of 74,000 'old moustaches' was animated by a passionate devotion to the Emperor and the feeling that this was the last desperate throw to decide the future of France. Despite a warning that if the battle was allowed to develop along the lines of the ones fought in the Peninsula it might lead to a disastrous result, Napoleon, who had never fought against Wellington, was determined to break up Wellington's mixed force by the hammer blows of massive columns. He tried all day, without success. 'How beautifully those English fight!' he said at one stage. 'But they *must* give way.' They very nearly did, but just as it looked as if the line might give, he was forced to divert men to meet the advance of Blücher and his Prussians. To make the last effort Napoleon sent forward the Old Guard which had never yet failed in an attack.

The Battle of Waterloo, the
final triumph of the line over
the column.

'Now, Maitland! Now's your time!' said the Duke to the commander of the British Brigade of Guards. Three hundred of the élite troops of the *Grande Armée* in their tall red-plumed bearskins fell in the first devastating volley. They staggered, stumbled and fell back, their right flank harassed by the fire of the 52nd Foot which had wheeled forward to take them in enfilade. The great moment came when Wellington raised his cocked hat and the whole line surged forward, down through the standing crops in the last irresistible charge which destroyed the *Grande Armée*, the French empire and all the hopes of its Emperor.

The Battle of Waterloo established Britain as the paramount military power in Europe. The prestige and influence gained for her by Wellington and his soldiers enabled the Foreign Secretary, Castlereagh, to dominate the Congress of Vienna – the peace conference. After twenty years of war the British army had reached its peak of efficiency, and was immediately broken up. The lustre of its reputation illuminated the political scene for the next generation, influencing the foreign policies of Castlereagh, Canning and Palmerston, and though solid enough in 1815, thereafter it was largely a myth. For the army, the period after Waterloo, known as the 'Great Peace', was one of total stagnation largely because Wellington, as a politician, actively opposed any form of progress or development.

To the Victorians, Waterloo put an end to the second Hundred Years War with France and to years of acute national danger. It introduced what everyone felt would be lasting peace, progress and prosperity because there was now no other European power capable of interfering with the development of the great Empire Britain had won. Yet, although there was peace in Europe for the next forty years, the main reason for military stagnation, the army was constantly employed in a long series of colonial campaigns. The First Burmese War of 1824–6 began only nine years after Waterloo; in South Africa the border wars in British Kaffraria and the fighting along the Fish River on the eastern boundary of Cape Colony which had first broken out in 1799, went on intermittently for nearly a hundred years. The First Afghan War, the First Chinese War, the First New Zealand War and costly campaigns against Punjabis, Mahrattas and Sikhs were all fought in the era of the Great Peace. In 1840 four-fifths of the army was stationed abroad; there were 59 battalions in the colonies, 22 in India, China and Burma, and only 22 at home.

Unfortunately for the politicians, merchants and taxpayers of Britain, who had no wish to support a standing army of 100,000 men – an unprecedented figure in peacetime – the mere existence of garrisons overseas perpetuated territorial expansion by a process no one seemed able to halt. The First Burmese War was a case in point. The King of Ava (or Burma) and his army, who had had some success in snatching the property of their neighbours and whose

THE BRITISH ATLAS, or John Bull supporting the Peace Establishment.

The attitude of the British taxpayer to the regular army.

delusions of invincibility were equalled only by their ignorance of Britain's resources, deliberately made so much trouble on the borders of British India, despite all the appeals and warnings of the Governor-General, Lord Amherst, the son of the conqueror of Canada, that an expedition was sent to enforce good behaviour. Thus Britain reluctantly acquired Burma. The same sequence of events was repeated again and again in India. Potentates on the borders either interfered or threatened to interfere with trade or security in British territories, or local people appealed for protection

The Storming Column
entering the great fortress of
Ghuznee in Afghanistan
before daybreak on
23 July 1839.

from the exactions of a despot. Military action was taken, this extended the boundaries of British rule, and within a few years the whole process was repeated.

British strategy swung far away from the 'cock-pit of Europe' and an interest in the commercial significance of the Scheldt, and centred upon India. In the eighteenth century the 'life-line' of the British Empire ran across the Atlantic to the islands of the West Indies and the colonies of North America. In the nineteenth century it ran due south to the Cape of Good Hope – Cape Town had been taken from the Dutch in 1806 – and then north-eastwards to India, regarded as the 'brightest jewel in the Imperial crown'. Napoleon had demonstrated the vulnerability of the more direct route (through the Mediterranean, across the Isthmus of Suez and down the Red Sea) when he went to Egypt in 1798. This road to the East lay under the threat of hostile elements in the decrepit Ottoman Empire. It was also menaced by French attempts to re-establish a presence in the Near East, Russian designs on Turkey and, above all, by Russian expansion into the Mediterranean through the Bosporus and the Dardanelles. The opening of the Suez Canal in 1869 merely increased Britain's concern and interest in the Near East, for the canal became a major factor in Imperial strategy, although the problems attached to this line of communication had existed for more than a century.

The Battle of Ferozeshah in the Punjab, India, 1845.

It was because of India that Britain became involved in what was known as 'the Eastern Question', the very complicated story of the plans cherished by so many European nations for the disposal of the Ottoman Empire; and it was because of India, and Russian intentions concerning the route through the Near East and Afghanistan, that in 1854 Britain, in an alliance with Turkey, France and Sardinia, became involved in the Crimean War. The main object of the Allies in going to war was to prevent Russia from establishing herself in Constantinople (Istanbul).

In the meantime the regiments of Britain's colonial army had added many new Battle Honours to their Colours, and names such as Ava (1824–6), Ghuznee (July 1839), Khelat (November 1839), Kabul (January 1842), Ferozeshah (December 1845), Aliwal (January 1846), Sobraon (February 1846) and Chilianwala (January 1849) appeared in regimental histories.

From the soldier's point of view little had changed since the Napoleonic Wars. He was now provided with one pound of bread and three-quarters of a pound of meat each day, and a generous government also supplied two large cooking-vessels per company mess in which the meat could be boiled. In 1854 a third 'daily meal' was provided, but the soldier had to pay for it. His pay was still one shilling a day, and three shillings and sixpence were deducted each

The Recruit. A bemused young man is persuaded to enter a life of glory and glamour while in the background (right) sits a shattered, wooden-legged veteran, the product of that life.

week to pay for food over and above the issue of bread and meat. Further stoppages of one shilling and tenpence halfpenny a week were made for laundry and 'general maintenance'. He was thus left with twopence three farthings a day to spend on himself, although 'barrack damages' and 'deficiencies' often extorted by Quartermaster-Sergeants, still had to be paid for. Practically his only relaxation was drinking in the wet canteen – if he had any money. Only men who were desperate joined the army, but it did at least offer shelter, clothing and food of a sort to Irishmen starving because of the Potato Famine.

No officer could maintain himself without a private income, and practically all officers lived in the regimental mess. Here everyone knew his own place within the exclusive circle where conduct and beliefs were governed by the rigid code of things done, and things not done. Courses of instruction, particularly those at the Senior Department of the Royal Military College, were not well attended, and any officer who really wanted to study his profession was considered slightly deranged. In the tight tactical formations of 'line' to receive infantry attacks, and 'square' to repel cavalry, no initiative or intelligence was required. In all the colonial wars it was courage

and determination that mattered; an officer had to have 'character', nothing more.

In the campaigns overseas, despite the occasional disaster such as the slaughter by the Afghans of the whole garrison of Kabul during the retreat of 1842, when only one man, Dr Brydon, reached safety at Jellalabad, the army was well enough equipped and organized to deal with its problems. Its uniform was substantially the same as it had worn at Waterloo, it still carried muzzle-loading muskets of much the same pattern that had been used for nearly 150 years, but while it was only required to fight local wars against natives it could meet the demands made on it. It was not designed to undertake a continental campaign against a great European power simply because in the opinion of the politicians – especially the ageing Duke of Wellington who ruled at Horse Guards from 1842 until his death at the age of eighty-three in 1852 – the Battle of Waterloo and its effect on British prestige had put an end to the era of British involvement in continental wars.

This prestige was shown to be a myth by the administrative chaos of the Crimean War (1854–6). There was nothing new about the disorganization: many times before, the British soldier and his

Cavalry officers of 1820. Their function, according to *Punch* some years later, was to give a little tone to what would otherwise be a vulgar brawl.

The General Officers
commanding in the Crimea.
Lord Raglan (left) – who had
been on Wellington's staff in
the Peninsula – faces the
French General Pélissier;
Omar Pasha is in the centre.

Opposite: the war in the
Crimea was the first in which
the appalling hardships
suffered by the army became
widely known and the public
conscience was awakened.
Above: Florence Nightingale
in Scutari Hospital. The
wards were much more
overcrowded than this
idealized picture suggests.
*Below: Huts and Warm
Clothing for the Army;* a
lithograph by W. Simpson
illustrating conditions in the
Crimea.

officers had suffered appalling hardships which were the direct result
of the corruption and incompetence of those who sent them to war.
But this time, because of steamships, railways and newspapers, the
facts became known and the public conscience was awakened. Much
of the credit for this must be given to the war correspondents,
although the breaches of ordinary military security by such men as
the notorious William Howard Russell of *The Times* cost countless
lives. 'We have no need of spies,' said the Tsar. 'We have *The Times.*'
    Russell's despatches were sent back to England by fast steamship
which brought the Crimea closer in time than Lisbon had been
during the Peninsular War. A remarkably efficient railway system
enabled newspapers to be distributed overnight and the Victorian
householder could read at breakfast of the sufferings of the army.
Social reform and great advances in medicine and hygiene, new
ideas on social administration and improvements in industrial
efficiency were overcoming much of the disease, filth and incompetence in civilian life, and now suddenly all the horrors of the
antiquated and long-neglected military system came to light. For
the first time the ordinary citizen of the prosperous middle classes,
who for centuries had known nothing and cared less about the

misery of the men who had so often protected him and his commercial interests in time of trouble, learned what was happening inside the army, and the knowledge struck him squarely in his conscience. The status of the army in the eyes of the nation began to change. A tide of reform began to flow, albeit slowly at first, through every department of the military organization.

Not for the first time, British soldiers and their regimental officers won a war against all the odds created for them by the incompetence of the command and supply system. They fought and won three great battles: at the Alma, when they drove the troops of Prince Aleksandr Menshikov off the heights south of the river with the bayonet (September 1854), at Balaclava in the following month, and at Inkerman in November. Balaclava is famous chiefly for the Charge of the Light Brigade under Lord Cardigan which prompted General Pierre Bosquet to remark, 'C'est magnifique, mais ce n'est pas la guerre'; the far more successful Charge of the Heavy Brigade on the same day is not so well remembered. Inkerman is known as the 'soldiers' battle', when a Russian attempt to break the Anglo-French siege of Sevastopol was repulsed in savage hand-to-hand fighting by a small Allied force. Although the main Russian armies had not been defeated, the war ended with the fall of Sevastopol

The grief and the glory.
Left: British war-wounded
brought back to London
from the Crimea. *Below:*
The 42nd at the Battle of the
Alma, 1854.

on 11 September 1855, after a long siege. The war had not solved the Eastern Question but it had checked Russian influence in south-eastern Europe.

Meanwhile in England the process of military reform had begun. At midnight on 29 January 1855 the House of Commons divided on a motion by John Arthur Roebuck Q.C., Radical Member for Sheffield, that a Select Committee should inquire into conditions in the army. In the debate the Secretary at War, Sydney Herbert, had been unwise enough to state that 'the responsibility [for the administrative chaos] lies with that collection of regiments which calls itself the British Army, and not with the Government.' Since the House rarely upholds an attempt to pass responsibility downwards the government fell, as Gladstone said, 'with such a thwack that you could hear their heads thump as they struck the ground'.

The Roebuck Committee then sat for several months investigating the causes of administrative failure, and this committee was followed by a plethora of similar inquiries. Between 1855 and the Esher Committee of 1904 there were no less than 567 commissions and committees of various sorts. Naturally, as the years passed, the zeal of the reformers abated somewhat, but the reports of all the hundreds of subsidiary inquiries, which examined the army as if through a microscope, did at least serve one useful purpose. By appearing at frequent intervals in the Press they kept alive an interest in service matters and made it impossible for politicians and the public to forget, as they had done during the Great Peace, that an army contains human beings who need protection against idle, corrupt and incompetent administrators.

By 1868 a mass of information on the military system had been collected. Though several attempts had been made at various times to revise the recruiting system, nothing much had been achieved. Until 1847 men had enlisted for life, thereafter the enlistment period was reduced to twenty-one years. Thus the ranks became filled with elderly drunkards and there was no reserve from which to augment or raise new units in an emergency. The Army Reserve Act of 1867 was a misguided compromise aimed at creating the reserve which had long been available to continental armies through conscription, but without introducing compulsory service. It was not a great success.

Other departmental reforms in the system and supply of rations, clothing, munitions and accommodation were also put into effect, but there remained a division of responsibilities between the Commander-in-Chief and the Secretary at War. This was not sorted out until Gladstone's great reforming administration came into office in 1868, and Edward Cardwell became the Liberal Secretary of State for War. He brought in three major reforms: the Army Enlistment Act of 1870, the Regulation of the Forces Act of 1871, and the scheme of 1872 which linked battalions of a regiment so as to ensure regular exchanges between home and overseas stations, and

THE ARMY OF THE FUTURE.

DEDICATED TO THOSE WHO WOULD IMPROVE ITS POSITION, BUT ARE AFRAID TO PAY THE PROPER PRICE.

A cartoon from *Fun* magazine, 1876. The cartoonists and newspapers, who for so long had reviled the army and all its ways, begin at last to realize that the soldier is a human being.

gave each regiment a county affiliation and a recruiting and training depot within its county.

The Army Enlistment Act created a reserve by requiring a man to sign on for six years with the Colours and six with the reserve, and this Act was connected with one which authorized the discharge from the army of men of bad character. The Regulation of the Forces Act abolished the system of purchase, and the scheme of 1872 not only ensured a reasonable rotation of battalions in home service and duties overseas but, by creating a firm association between militia and regular units in a localized area, stimulated recruiting, did much to bridge the gap between citizen and soldier, and aroused local pride in the record and achievements of the county regiment.

Cardwell also reorganized army administration by the War Office Act of 1870 and various subsequent Orders in Council. The Commander-in-Chief, a soldier, was subordinated to the Secretary for War, a politician, and the Secretary of State was not only made

H.R.H. the Duke of Cambridge (*left*), Commander-in-Chief of the army, who successfully blocked many of the reforms proposed by Cardwell (*right*), the Liberal Secretary of State for War.

directly responsible for every branch of the army but his personal estate could be held forfeit in the event of corruption or malpractice. The War Office and Horse Guards were amalgamated and their functions distributed among three executive departments: that of the Commander-in-Chief, responsible for the purely military aspects of all the armed land forces of the Crown; that of the Surveyor-General (later Master-General) of the Ordnance dealing with all supply and equipment; and that of the Financial Secretary who was directly responsible to the Secretary for War for all matters concerning pay, accounting, estimates and expenditure.

Some of Cardwell's measures and many of his proposals encountered opposition so firmly entrenched that they could not be put into effect. For example, he was anxious to curb the personal power of the Commander-in-Chief and institute a General Staff based on the Prussian pattern, but H.R.H. the Duke of Cambridge, cousin of the Queen, was the Commander-in-Chief and he resolutely refused to sacrifice one iota of his hitherto unchallenged control of the army. The Queen and the Court supported him and he was able to hang on for another twenty-five years, growing ever more stubbornly resistant to change and reform as the years went by.

In the Indian Mutiny of 1857, which led to the transfer of power in the subcontinent from the East India Company to the Crown on 1 September 1858, in General Napier's expedition to Abyssinia of 1868, and in the Sudan War (1881–99), the fighting followed the pattern of earlier colonial campaigns. Soldiers fought in scarlet tunics and relied on massed volleys fired at short range from infantry squares. But technological progress, particularly in the fields of metallurgy and design, was having a profound effect on the development of weapons which, in conjunction with the invention of smokeless powder, affected tactics.

Although there had been experiments in breech-loading and rifling ever since the sixteenth century it had never before been technically possible to produce either a gas-tight breech, or a system of locking the breech so that it would not burst or blow off and kill the firer. Nor had it been possible to devise an easily manufactured and reliable method of loading and firing. A Frenchman named Pauly found that the breech could be sealed by the expansion of a soft metal base on a cartridge at the moment of detonation, and Johann von Dreyse, a German, developed a breech with a bolt action which enabled the firer to slide a round into the chamber, lock the bolt and at the same time cock the trigger mechanism. The trigger, when operated, released a spring which sent a long needle

Colonial wars: the storming of the Kashmire Gate, Delhi, India, 1857.

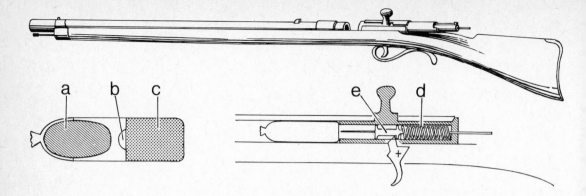

a, b, c, e, d

The earliest mass-produced breech-loading rifles, the German 'needle-gun' (*above*) and the later French Chassepot rifle (*below*).

a, bullet; *b*, priming charge; *c*, propellant; *d*, firing spring; *e*, 'needle' or pin firing mechanism.

through the cartridge and exploded the charge placed behind the bullet. The spent round was ejected when the bolt was opened. Known as the 'needle-gun', Dreyse's weapon was issued to the Prussian army in 1843. It was the first mass-produced breech-loading rifle to come into service, and since it had a rate of fire six times faster than the old muzzle-loader, and could be fired by a man lying down behind cover, it enabled the Prussians to annihilate the solid formations of the Austrian army in the war of 1866. Suddenly the whole long-established edifice of close order drill and massed volleys collapsed.

By 1870 the French had greatly improved on the needle-gun with their Chassepot rifle, which was far more reliable and had three times the range. Sights could now be calibrated up to 1,000 yards. Weapon development leapt ahead. The Prussians produced breech-loading rifled field artillery which far outranged the French muzzle-loading smooth-bores in the war of 1870. The French invented the *mitrailleuse*, a machine-gun working on the principle of hand-rotated multiple barrels and adopted by the British in the form developed by the American, Dr Gatling. It had ten barrels and could fire 500 rounds in a minute. In 1884 Hiram Maxim invented the first really automatic single-barrelled weapon. This used the gases from

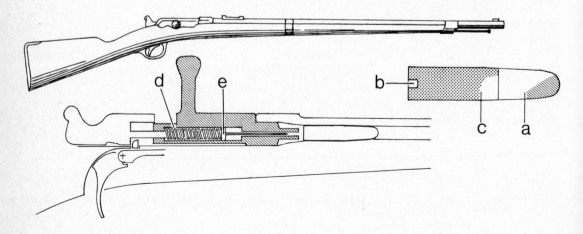

A Maxim gun crew on the North-West Frontier, c. 1898. The Maxim was the first fully automatic, belt-fed machine-gun.

the exploding rounds to operate the breech mechanism which fed rounds from a belt into the breech, and fired and ejected them when the firer maintained pressure on the trigger plate. The Maxim gun, firing between 450 and 500 rounds (two belts) a minute at ranges up to a mile and a half, was adopted by the British army in 1889. The improved Vickers-Maxim, with very slight modifications thereafter, was used in the Boer War and both World Wars. Machine-gunners were wont to call it the 'Queen of the Battlefield', and for the first time since the Battle of Agincourt the infantry had a weapon comparable in range and effect to the 'arrow-storm'.

The evolution of weapons was not the only military advance in the years after the Crimean War. The first practical electric telegraph had been set up between Euston and Chalk Farm (London) in 1837, and the system was used for military purposes between London and the Crimea in the war of 1854. The first public railway, between Stockton-on-Tees and Darlington in England, had been opened in 1825. Within a few years it became possible to move an army's supplies in great bulk and at a speed of twenty miles an hour instead of fifteen miles a day. It seemed as if the day of the messenger on his horse and the horse-drawn wagon had gone for ever. Orders and information, scaled down to the limitations of transmission by the telegraph in the code invented by Samuel B. Morse and Alfred Vail, could now be passed swiftly over great distances, and the railway linked armies in the field with all the manpower and material resources of the nations they represented.

Yet there were many countries in which the British army was called upon to fight where these two great advances in communications could not be exploited for many years. In any case, the traditional parsimoniousness of British governments in military matters always delayed the introduction of new ideas. Even in 1941 the transport resources of a British infantry battalion in the Indian station of Allahabad were seven horses, thirty-five mules and four AT (Animal Transport) mule-drawn carts.

It also seemed that with these developments in weapons and communications the era of 'professional' wars, fought by comparatively small professional forces for limited political or territorial aims, had ended too. Karl von Clausewitz, who in his book *Vom Kriege* brought up to date the principles of war expounded by the great military writer of the fourth century BC, Sun Tzu, in the classic *Art of War*, wrote that future wars would be national conflicts, fought to the death using all the resources of the whole nation. Clausewitz (1780–1831) based his opinion on the French Revolutionary and Napoleonic Wars. These were certainly ideological in motive, maintained by conscription, requiring the total involvement of the nations concerned, and had the unlimited aim of complete victory. He was right so far as the American Civil War of 1861–5 was concerned, but in Europe his prophecy was not fulfilled until 1914.

Chapter Five

SOUTH AFRICA AND FLANDERS

Britain's army, keeping the peace and every now and again extending the local borders of the Empire, became more and more
separated from the European concept of war during the latter part
of the nineteenth century. The Franco-Prussian War of 1870 had
been an unpleasant warning of what could happen if Britain allowed
herself to become involved in continental politics, and so she turned
her back on old enemies and allies and concentrated on a policy
of strategic expansion which, in Europe, was labelled imperialist
aggression.

The Zulu War of 1879 had the aim of taking possession of Zulu-
land on the grounds that the magnificent Zulu army, created by
Chief Chaka in 1816, was a menace to the security of British
settlers in Natal. The initial disaster at Isandhlwana, when 21 officers
and 534 soldiers of the 24th Regiment were overrun by the main
Zulu army of 20,000 men, was partially redeemed by the extraordinary defence of the mission station at Rorke's Drift, on the

The heroic defence of
Rorke's Drift in the Zulu
War, 1879.

Chief Langalebela and his sons after capture in the Zulu War, 1879.

Buffalo River, where 140 men of the 24th Regiment, many of them sick, drove off the attacks of a Zulu 'impi' of 4,000 men in a fight lasting from four o'clock on a January afternoon until four o'clock the next morning. Eleven Victoria Crosses were awarded for this action. Lord Chelmsford, the British commander of a reconstituted invasion force, finally destroyed Chief Cetewayo's Zulu army at Ulundi.

Sir Garnet Wolseley's advance up the Nile in 1885 had the object of rescuing General Gordon, besieged in Khartoum by Sudanese Mahdists, but it was only a phase in the Sudan War which began in 1881 and ended in 1899. The underlying aim was to secure the Sudan. The relieving force reached Khartoum forty-eight hours after the murder of Gordon who, afflicted with a death-wish, had never really tried to escape. On the approach march this force of 1,800 men had had to fight a savage battle at Abu Klea against 10,000 'Fuzzy-Wuzzies' under the Mahdi's Lieutenant Mohammed Ahmed. For the first time in any of the many colonial wars a native enemy broke a British square.

Three years later the army was issued with a new rifle, the ·303 inch Lee-Metford, fitted with a magazine capable of holding ten rounds.

A spring in the base of the magazine forced up each round in turn to the level of the chamber, so that the firer merely had to operate the bolt to eject a spent round and feed another into the breech. These rifles, capable of sustained rapid fire in the hands of a well-trained man, had a killing range of 2,000 yards and were extremely accurate.

Rifled artillery, with its infinitely greater range and accuracy, the machine-gun and the long-range rifle ended for ever the battlefield drills which had persisted right up to the Battle of Omdurman in 1898. Even so, the British army remained, as always, dangerously conservative in its outlook, and despite the lessons learned at so great a cost in the Boer War there were still senior officers in 1916 who had not apparently advanced beyond the tactics of Frederick the Great.

The causes of the Boer War have been a matter of dispute among historians ever since the Boer army crossed the frontier into Natal on 12 October 1899. But undoubtedly an important factor behind the conflict was the earlier war against the Boers of 1881. Under the pretext of bringing law and order to the Boer Republic of the Transvaal, Britain had annexed it in 1877 and two years later declared it to be a Crown Colony. Since it was in an attempt to escape the hated British rule that the Boers had moved north in the Great Trek and established themselves on the northern side of the Vaal River, this aroused their bitterest feelings. They took up arms and defeated the British at Bronkhorstspruit, the Ingogo River, Laing's Nek and Majuba Hill, the first successful colonial revolt since the loss of the American Colonies. The British army was accustomed

The 'Fuzzy-Wuzzies' break the British square at Abu Klea in 1885.

to losing the opening battles in most of its wars, but this time Gladstone made peace so quickly – the war lasted only three months – that there was no time for it to redeem itself. The Transvaal was given its independence and the Boers, reasonably enough, developed an exaggerated idea of their own considerable abilities and a contempt for British troops. Overconfidence was to be their undoing.

By October 1899 they were convinced that another attempt was being made to drag them into the British Empire. So they attacked first, feeling sure that with 45,000 men they could drive the 20,000 British garrison troops into the sea before reinforcements could arrive from India or England. Despite local initial defeats at Talana Hill and Dundee on 20 October, at Elandslaagte on the following day, and a repulse at Mafeking after their bombardment on 23 October, they did succeed in bottling up most of the available British forces in Kimberley, Mafeking and Ladysmith, thus making these three towns the focal points of the inevitable British counter-attack. This was mounted by General Sir Redvers Buller who had made his considerable military reputation in the Red River expedition in Canada in 1869–70 and the Second Ashanti War of 1873–4. He came out from England and divided the relieving force he brought with him into three columns. One, under General Lord Methuen, had Kimberley as its objective. In the centre, General Gateacre was

A Second Balaclava Charge, the charge of the 21st Lancers during the Battle of Omdurman, 1898.

Balloon used for scouting in the Boer War. Observation balloons were first employed on Sir James Baird's march across the desert from Port Sudan to Alexandria in 1801.

to relieve Mafeking, far to the north, and Buller himself proposed to take the eastern column to Ladysmith.

Gateacre marched boldly towards Mafeking, and since his enemies were only Boers and amateur soldiers, he did not waste time over precautions such as cavalry patrols to protect his advance. The Boers lay in wait for him at Stormberg, where he lost 700 men and was forced to retreat. Methuen, refusing to believe information given to him by a colonial scout and a local Kaffir, launched a night attack over ground he had not reconnoitred, fell into a Boer trap, lost 1,000 men and withdrew. Buller sent his men across open country against Boers skilfully entrenched at Colenso, suffered the loss of 12 Royal Artillery guns and 1,100 casualties, and fell back. This trinity of disasters, Stormberg on 10 December, Magersfontein on 11 December and Colenso on 15 December 1899, became known as 'Black Week'. British commanders had failed to appreciate the

tactical implications of modern weapons and ammunition in the
hands of marksmen who had grown up with a hunting-rifle in
their hands.

Buller was replaced by Lord Roberts, who received the instruction
to take over the command in South Africa on the same day that
news came of the death of his only son, killed while trying to save
the guns at Colenso. Roberts, who had gained much experience of
guerrilla fighting in Abyssinia, Afghanistan, India and Burma,
appreciated the value of 'a man on a horse' in a country so vast as
South Africa. Taking Kitchener with him to be his Chief of Staff
he went out to his new command, reorganized the army and
equipped it to meet the local conditions, raised units of mounted
infantry, and began his campaign with the relief of Kimberley.
The Boer General Piet Cronje was defeated at Paardeberg; the
Transvaal and Orange Free State were invaded and Pretoria and
Johannesburg occupied. Finally, pinned up against the borders of
Basutoland, the Boer army under Prinsloo capitulated; by 1 September 1900 the principal Boer towns were all in British hands,
secure lines of communication had been established, and by all the
rules the fighting should have been over. Lord Roberts certainly
thought so. He handed over his command to Kitchener and went
home, having done what he had been asked to do.

Opposite: mobile war in
South Africa. *Above:* Boer
commandos armed with
Mauser rifles. Note the
crossed bandoliers capable of
holding up to 300 rounds – a
formidable weight to carry
on mobile operations. *Below:*
Australian scouts on tandem
rail bicycles now preserved
in the museum at Pretoria.

Connecting Trench and wire fence
between blockhouses (109 & 110)
Kroonstadt – Lindley

But the Boers went on fighting. The war dragged on for another eighteen months while Kitchener gradually wore down the elusive and fast-moving Boer commandos with his policy of scorched earth, attrition and concentration camps – a term which then had none of its more modern connotations.

The war had a profoundly disturbing effect in Britain. Warmed by the glow of Victorian peace and prosperity (for some) Great Britain, in her policies and general attitude, had drifted away from Europe into a state of Imperial isolation. She now discovered it had taken practically all the resources of her regular army, supplemented by many of the militia battalions and strong contingents from Australia, New Zealand and Canada to assert her authority over a few Dutch farmers. The Boer War had shown the rest of the world how weak the military resources of the British Empire really were.

The threat of war had been increasing slowly in Europe for years, and the continental nations had been perfecting plans for mobilizing their manpower and material resources against the day, which many believed would come soon, when they would be called upon to fight for survival. France, Germany, Russia and Austria numbered their regular and reserve manpower in millions. Germany was building a battle fleet. Without any warning she had emerged as a rival and as a potential enemy. The complacency imparted by forty years of peace while the Queen Empress governed nearly a quarter of the globe gave way to considerable alarm, and at the turn of the century the people of Britain found themselves facing much the same problems that had had to be faced in the sixteenth and eighteenth centuries. Their weakness was known and they had no allies in Europe.

Little had been done in the way of army reform since the days of Edward Cardwell, though in 1881 one of his successors, Hugh

Blockhouse 109.

Childers, completed the linked battalion scheme by amalgamating
units in regiments of two battalions and replacing the old numbers
with county and other titles. However, one of the beneficial results
of Cardwell's reform had been to raise the status of soldiering;
the criminals and habitual drunkards had gone from the ranks. Yet
the centuries-old prejudice still lingered, and because of the miserable
pay and conditions – plenty of barracks were far worse than prisons
in terms of space allowed to a man – the army was still only a refuge
for unfortunates. The majority of recruits joined because of chronic
unemployment or to escape from trouble of various sorts at home.
Thus, inevitably, many soldiers were ignorant, unintelligent and
physically of a low standard. Discipline had to be strict, and though
such men were capable of great endurance and courage – of which
they gave countless examples – they were on the whole entirely
dependent on their officers. When separated from them they showed
little initiative or response to a situation and were bad at looking
after themselves. They had changed little since Marlborough's day.

Officers had changed very little too, in outlook and behaviour, over
the previous hundred years. They came from the upper classes of
society, and the need for a private income and an unofficial system of
pre-selection by regimental representatives at Sandhurst acted as
filters to ensure that young men entering a regiment were all of
much the same type. Only quartermasters came from the ranks. A
second lieutenant or ensign was paid eight shillings a day. Promotion was by vacancy. Battalions had a fixed establishment of majors,
captains, lieutenants and second lieutenants, and since there was
practically no staff organization, and thus very little opportunity
for an officer to serve outside his regiment, many remained in it
until retirement or death took them away. When this happened,
everyone moved up one place. In these circumstances it was not

SOCIAL LIFE IN THE ARMY.

ILLUSTRATIONS BY G.M. PAYNE.

100 UP.

UNDER CANVAS.
A CANTEEN CONCERT.

AT THE SERGEANTS
BALL.

AT THE REGIMENTAL SPORTS.

CHURCH PARADE.

A SOLDIER'S WEDDING IN INDIA.

ON THE STRENGTH.

unusual for second lieutenants to remain in that rank for eighteen or twenty years, waiting for dead men's shoes. There was a stigma attached to serving outside the regiment, and it was generally considered that to be 'on the staff' indicated that either an officer was undesirably keen or his regiment did not want him. Ambition centred on command of a battalion; to go further was often largely a matter of luck – being in the right place at the right time – and influence. The method of assessing the professional capabilities of officers by the annual confidential report was unreliable since most of their time was spent playing polo, racing, hunting, shooting and fishing. The code was strict. In the mess it was forbidden to talk shop, discuss religion or mention a woman's name. After a long, dusty route march it was unthinkable – in a good regiment – for an officer to have a drink or even sit down until he had inspected his men's feet and made certain all his soldiers had a proper meal.

The army was not a great burden on the taxpayer. The men were paupers and officers had to have money of their own. It was a cheap way to run an Empire. Intellectual ability was regarded with suspicion. Junior officers were not encouraged to display initiative. Training was based on the reduction of practically every military function to a simple drill, and on developing immediate and unquestioning obedience to orders. 'You are not paid to think' was the oft-repeated rebuke intended to keep junior officers and all N.C.O.s in their place.

Yet, because of smokeless powder and long-range weapons, all the old tactical principles and indeed the whole pattern of war had changed. Up to now, although the soldier had had to stand unflinching and resolute under enemy fire, he could find some comfort and gain moral support from the nearness of his comrades and his officers in the close formation. The Boer War had taught him he could no longer go forward in the mass, loading and firing volleys whenever the orders were given. The Germans had realized this in 1888 and their training after that date envisaged attacks made by small bodies of troops, well spread out in open order, moving forward in short rushes under covering fire of artillery and machine-guns from one piece of cover to the next, with no rigid tactical drills. The soldier was now an individual with the far more frightening task of moving against an enemy he could not see but whose bullets he could hear. Success in battle would depend on the alertness and initiative of every officer and man, and their ability to shoot, observe, move, conceal themselves and stay alive.

It was a complete revolution in military thinking. The French would have none of it. To them, moral superiority was the decisive factor and this could only be demonstrated by the headlong frontal attack which would paralyse defenders. For them the great days of the Imperial Guard, the 'old moustaches', had not passed.

Britain's military leaders came to no definite tactical conclusions, but on one aspect of training there was no dispute. The lesson of

Opposite: a somewhat idealized representation of a sergeant's life in the army – but a great step forward in recognizing that the soldier could play his part in 'civilized' society.

The Short Magazine
Lee-Enfield (SMLE) rifle,
No. 1 Mk III ·303; the
soldier's personal weapon in
the First and Second
World Wars.

Black Week could be expressed in one word: musketry. When the
old President of the Transvaal, Paul Kruger, had said, 'the Boers can
shoot, and that is everything', he had given the reason for the
British defeats. Thereafter the British army concentrated on
perfecting its skill with the new Lee-Enfield rifle, and attained so
high a standard that in the famous retreat from Mons in 1914
German field intelligence reported that the British battalion
establishment of machine-guns was twenty-eight. In fact, it was two.

Even before the Boer War it had been clear to such men as Sir
Garnet Wolseley that the British army was still in no state to go to
war against a major continental power, but the whole military
system lay inert under the hand of the elderly Duke of Cambridge,
determined to resist all change. In 1890 the Hartingdon Committee
recommended the formation of a Committee of Imperial Defence,
abolition of the post of Commander-in-Chief, formation of a
General Staff, and the placing of all responsibility for the army in
the hands of an Army Council. This was to consist of ministers, the
Permanent Under-Secretary, the Chief of the General Staff,
Adjutant-General, Quartermaster-General, Director of Artillery
and Inspector-General of Fortifications. But it was fourteen years
before these reforms could be put into effect, even though the Duke
of Cambridge was at last eased out of authority in 1895.

In the spring of 1904 the Report of the War Office (Reconstitution)
Committee, better known as the Esher Report, was published. Its
analysis of military administration, and its recommendations for the
proper organization of the War Office and the setting up of a
General Staff system were accepted by the government and put into
effect. At last, and in the nick of time, a functional staff structure
was built. This was not only the foundation for a reorganization of
the army as a whole but it made possible the vast expansion of the
land forces in the First and Second World Wars. Other vital recommendations of the Esher Committee included the vertical division of
responsibility through every level of command, so that, for example,
administrative decisions taken at the top were handled only by
administrative staff officers at all stages. Training was to be separated
from administration, and administrative districts were to be set up
throughout the country, which would take over the functions of
administration and organization and leave the field force units free
to train for war.

Lord Haldane, another of the great reformers.

These recommendations were implemented by Richard Burdon Haldane, the Liberal Secretary for War who took office in 1906, and it was primarily his intellectual capabilities and sustained hard work which, during the next three years, turned the War Office and the General Staff into an efficient and effective machine. With the 'Haldane Reforms', he also completed the task which had defeated his predecessors, the reorganization of the regular and reserve armies.

Implementation of the Esher Report involved the retraining of all the land forces in every aspect of tactics, administration and staff work; and the influence of the new General Staff, which gave an entirely fresh impetus to the Staff College and all training establishments, inspired the whole army with a sense of professionalism and purpose which had not existed since Oliver Cromwell's time.

Thus, when the First World War began in the summer of 1914, general mobilization and the move of the British Expeditionary Force (the B.E.F.) were operations conducted with extraordinary smoothness and efficiency. This came as a surprise to all those who presumed, with sound historical precedents, that once again the government and the army would be caught unawares and unprepared. Rolleston West, a young subaltern of the Intelligence Corps crossing to France on 13 August at the time when two army corps were moving to their pre-arranged positions in France, recorded in his diary 'the astonishing completeness of it all'. It was the result of meticulous planning and preparation by all departments of the reorganized staff.

All this reorganization, training, planning and preparation were about to be tested in battles which, in terms of troops involved, frontages and casualties, dwarfed all previous campaigns in history. No one, on either side, had any experience of handling such huge forces in battle.

'Fifty years were spent in the process of making Europe explosive,' wrote Liddell Hart in his *History of the World War*, 'five days were enough to detonate it.' The armies went to war with Horse, Foot and Guns, much as they had always done, but whereas continental cavalry was trained for the charge with lance or sabre, the roles of British cavalry were primarily reconnaissance, and skirmishing to prevent the enemy from reconnoitring. In the world of intelligence collection the B.E.F. had one entirely new asset in the Royal Flying Corps, and sixty-three aircraft flew across to the operational airfield at Maubeuge.

The strategists in Britain who had tried to plan for the coming war had assumed that since she was the greatest naval power in the world, Britain's role would be largely maritime. The Royal Navy would contain or destroy the German battle fleet and blockade Germany while the land forces of France and Russia, assisted by the B.E.F., dealt with the armies of Germany and Austria. It was a repetition of the maritime policy of both the Pitts, who had sought to avoid the problems and expense of a heavy military commitment on the Continent.

Germany's operations were based on the Schlieffen Plan, named after its originator, the Chief of Staff in 1906. Practically the whole German field force, organized in seven armies and totalling about

A Blériot monoplane on manœuvres, 1913. Aircraft introduced an entirely new factor into the collection of information. The balloon merely increased an observer's field of view; the pilot of an aeroplane could be tasked to provide specific information.

English postcard, 1914. Much propaganda was aimed at making the soldiers of opposing armies hate one another. It had far more effect on the civilians who did not have to endure trench warfare.

1,500,000 men, would advance through neutral Belgium and northern France on an enormous frontage extending from Aachen in the north to Strasbourg in the south. They would outflank the French defences in the north and then wheel south across the plains of Picardy and Champagne to take Paris. Everything depended on speed. When France had fallen the German armies would turn about and destroy the torpid Russians who were always slow in putting their forces into the field.

France intended to meet any German invasion with a massive counter-offensive in Lorraine.

Practically all the military experts in Europe were confident that the war would be over by Christmas; but German statesmen and industrialists did not share the optimism of the German General Staff, and in England Lord Kitchener, Chief of the General Staff, was almost alone in insisting that preparations be made for a long and bloody struggle. Kitchener was right, the strategists were wrong, and all the plans sank in the mud of the trenches.

Unlike other wars in the past, from the very beginning there was an extraordinary release of propaganda-fed international hatred, and great efforts were made to arouse a fighting spirit in the soldiers. It was the British propaganda services which put the phrase 'Britain's contemptible little army' into the mouth of Kaiser Wilhelm II, to describe what was undoubtedly the finest army Britain had ever sent overseas. The Kaiser himself never underestimated it, and von Kluck, who had to fight it, called it 'incomparable'.

Von Kluck, commanding the German First Army, entered Brussels on 20 August. Two days later the British and German armies made their first contact in a cavalry skirmish at Castreau, just north of Mons. On 23 August, instead of outflanking the little B.E.F. von Kluck blundered into it; Allenby's cavalry division had effectively prevented him from finding out where it was. In the

The Grenadier Guards at Mons, 1914. The 'Retreat from Mons' was awarded as a Battle Honour.

muddled Battle of Mons, fought among the slag-heaps of the mining district, the accurate rapid rifle-fire of the British infantry ripped into the dense formations of field-grey uniforms and momentarily stemmed the tide. But with the full weight of four German armies against them the French Fifth Army and the B.E.F., on the extreme left flank of the French, were compelled to fall back. The retreat from Mons lasted for a fortnight, and though Sir Horace Smith-Dorrien's corps of the B.E.F. once against checked von Kluck in a gallant delaying action fought on the line of the ridge at le Cateau, and the French even counter-attacked at Guise, the Allied forces were driven southwards beyond the Marne almost to the Seine, east of Paris.

But the Germans had overreached themselves. The Schlieffen Plan was too ambitious, and the German supreme commander, von Moltke, did not have enough troops to carry it out. Huge problems of communications and supply forced the German First Army to swing east of Paris, to shorten the line. Von Moltke's health and nerve broke down under the strain, and when Joffre launched the French Sixth Army in a general counter-offensive, the Battle of the Marne, in the first week of September, it was the turn of the Germans to retreat. It is conceivable that the Allies could have won a decisive battle on the Aisne in the following week had it not been for the arrival of a German reserve corps which had moved up by forced marches. Then began the 'Race to the Sea', for the port of Antwerp. In October and November both sides made furious efforts to outflank one another while there was still open ground for mobile

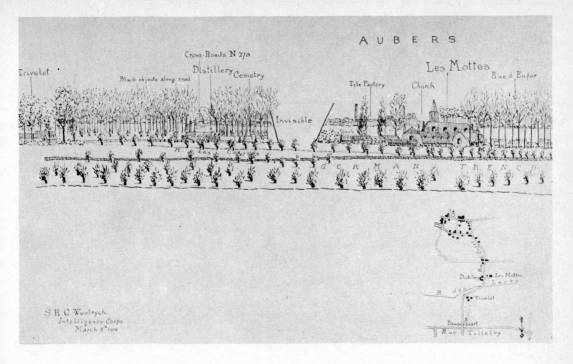

operations, and the head-on battles round Ypres were fought in the desperate hope of reaching a final decision and ending the war before the new year.

By this time the system of trenches, begun at the Aisne, had reached the Channel coast in the north, and ran south to the mountains of Switzerland. For the first time in the history of warfare a tactical situation had developed in which there were no flanks, and a war was to be fought in what Lord Wavell later described as 'conditions of siege'. Manœuvre was impossible while armies faced

Trench warfare; soldiers had to use periscopes (*left*) in order to obtain the accurate sketches of enemy front-line positions (*above*) so valuable for directing artillery fire and planning raids.

each other from unbroken lines of trenches, in places only a few yards apart, and all this had come about because war had ceased to be a purely professional matter and was now a national responsibility. Conscription and the organization of the reserve forces of continental nations had produced enough soldiers to hold a front of 400 miles.

Britain lagged far behind the continental nations in accepting the concept of war as a supreme national effort, and she now began to realize that the problems confronting her were formidable. It was clear that France could not be left to bear the military burden virtually alone, as she had done during the first six months of the war, but little had been done to mobilize the resources of the United Kingdom. Conscription had never been introduced because it was held to be incompatible with freedom and democracy. No one in authority, except Kitchener, had believed that the war could last long. (Kitchener, it is said, added in his own hand another nought to the figure of 50,000 suggested by his staff at the War Office for the expansion of the regular army in 1914.) There was no trained reserve of officers and N.C.O.s to form a nucleus for expansion, and in terms of clothing, equipment, accommodation and training facilities, everything had been scaled to meet the needs of an army of only 200,000 men.

Faced with an entirely unforeseen situation, Britain had to devote enormous effort to improvisation in order to create an army of 2,000,000 men. The famous Kitchener poster 'Your Country Needs YOU' appeared, and motivated by patriotism or the hope of adventure, or to escape from hunger and unemployment, 1,186,350 volunteers joined the Colours by the end of 1914. Even in this crisis the Liberal government would not resort to conscription. Unlike the expansion of the army in the wars of the eighteenth century, no new regiments were raised and the two-battalion regiments of the Cardwell system were expanded, in some cases, to as many as fifty battalions. Not the least of the problems in raising 'Kitchener's Army' was training. The regular army, the most obvious source of commanders and instructors, had been virtually destroyed in the battles of 1914; a typical example is that of the 1st Battalion of The Queen's Royal Regiment which crossed to France in the *Braemar Castle* on 12 August 1914 with a total of 998 all ranks. On 1 November, a few weeks later, the total strength was 2 corporals and 27 men. Gradually these fearful losses were replaced and the B.E.F. in the trenches of Flanders and Picardy slowly increased as regulars from overseas garrisons, territorials and special reservists came to join it. Despite these reinforcements, throughout 1915 Britain's contribution was only a very small part of the Allied force in France.

Both sides built up their strength and prepared for what all now knew would be a long war, and for the foreseeable future all the advantages lay with the Germans. The Schlieffen Plan had gained them a huge area of French territory, an occupation intolerable to

Lord Kitchener, Chief of the Imperial General Staff, speaking at a recruiting office in 1915.

all Frenchmen. To them, every yard snatched back was worth while, whereas to the Germans the sacrifice of low-lying ground in favour of commanding positions on high ground was merely tactical common sense. Thus the Germans invariably held the initiative and the Allies were committed to frontal attacks against enemy positions, sited in great depth, which were constantly being strengthened.

The greatest of the Allied problems was artillery ammunition. Unlike the Germans, the French and English were unable to convert industries swiftly to the production of munitions; Britain, having always relied on the German chemical industry, had practically no resources for the manufacture of explosives. The Allies were compelled to seek expensive help from America, but initially the quality of American ammunition was extremely poor. Shells were apt to explode in the gun, killing the crew, or fall short and cause casualties among Allied infantry, or merely fail to explode when they reached the target. Thus often enough artillery bombardments were nothing like as effective a prelude to an infantry attack as they should have been, and major offensives failed to make any progress against the fire of enemy machine-guns. The British launched two such offensives in 1915 – one in March at Neuve-Chapelle and Aubers

Ridge and the other in September at Loos – mainly to prove to the French that they were taking an active part in the war. The Germans had used poison gas for the first time at the Second Battle of Ypres in April, and the British used it at Loos, without any decisive effect. Throughout the year the French made constant attacks in Champagne and Artois, suffering a total of 1,500,000 casualties, yet the Allied offensives only established the basic fact that though local successes might be gained in the first advance, the momentum ceased as soon as the enemy realized what was happening. Thereafter any further attacks resulted in futile losses.

Even at the beginning of 1915 it had become clear that a breakthrough assault on a scale large enough to force the Germans to withdraw from northern France was beyond the capabilities of the Allied armies, and therefore Kitchener, prompted by Winston Churchill, resolved merely to hold the static lines in France while (in his own words) 'operations proceed elsewhere'. Turkey had now entered the war on the side of the Germans and Central Powers, and the operation Churchill and Kitchener had in mind was a landing on the Gallipoli peninsula and the capture of Constantinople (Istanbul). The idea was sound enough. Turkey might be knocked out of the war, a new threat to the Germans and Austrians in the

Opposite above: the Allies were short of artillery ammunition at the beginning of the war, but made sure that they had a sufficient stockpile (shown here, some of it camouflaged) before the Somme offensive in 1916.

Opposite below: a gas sentry sounding the gas alarm at Fleurbar, June 1916.

Gallipoli, 1915: a Turkish sniper (centre) just after capture.

Balkans might save Serbia, and the desperately needed warm-water supply route to Russia would be opened. The plan failed largely because a naval attempt to force the Dardanelles alerted the Turks, and despite heroic efforts the assaulting troops could make little progress against the same factors which dictated the course of operations on the Western Front: the trench system, barbed wire, the machine-gun and the artillery barrage. Fifty per cent of the troops employed became casualties and the peninsula was evacuated in January 1916.

At the end of 1915, mainly because of the failure of the Battle of Loos, Sir John French, the original commander of the B.E.F., was relieved by Sir Douglas Haig, who led the armies in France to final victory in 1918. This is often forgotten, and his achievements tend to be obscured by the accusations levelled against him for the slaughter of a generation on the Western Front. Perhaps his main fault was that he was apt, against his own judgment, to accept the advice of his specialist advisers such as Charteris, his Brigadier-General (Intelligence), and his army commanders. He was usually right and they were wrong. He was certainly wrong to accede to the proposals of General Sir Henry Rawlinson, commander of the Fourth Army, in the planning of the Battle of the Somme in the summer of 1916, for Rawlinson based everything on a disastrous misconception. He was convinced that the great break-through to decisive victory depended on neutralizing enemy positions with artillery-fire. A massive and prolonged bombardment would, so he said, 'leave nothing alive'. The infantry could march up to their objectives and 'would not need their rifles'. In fact the Germans emerged from their deep dugouts after a bombardment which had lasted a week and had failed even to cut their wire, and their machine-guns mowed down the long lines of advancing infantry in swathes. At a cost of 60,000 casualties on the first day of the battle (1 July) the Allied front, forty miles wide, moved forward barely one mile, and any hope of a great victory, to be exploited by General Gough's reserve army of three cavalry divisions, died with the men who fell on the chalk downs below the German trenches. The battle that was to have ended the war was decided on that first day yet it went on until November. By that time the Allied casualty-list had risen to more than 600,000 men. Truly was it said by Liddell Hart that the Somme was the glory and the graveyard of Kitchener's Army.

It was in this battle that Haig first used tanks, although on a scale too small to be really effective. Out of a total of 49, 15 failed to reach the assembly area and only 18 went into action. Yet this new weapon was far more decisive in its influence on the war than

The front line, Ovillers, during the Battle of the Somme, July 1916. All the dirt, discomfort and exhaustion of trench warfare are in this picture.

Tanks were first used during the Battle of the Somme, though on too small a scale to be effective. *Left:* a Mark I tank of 'C' Company in Chimpanzee Valley on 15 September 1916 – the day tanks first went into action, except for this one which broke down. Note the flimsy 'anti-shell netting' on the top. *Below:* the first tanks had a semaphore apparatus rigged on the top, which lasted about three minutes under shellfire. Pigeons were the only reliable means of passing information back; there was no means of communicating *to* a tank in action, apart from opening the hatch and shouting.

MILITARY SERVICE ACT
1916

EVERY UNMARRIED MAN
of
MILITARY AGE
Not excepted or exempted under this Act
CAN CHOOSE
ONE OF TWO COURSES:

(1) He can ENLIST AT ONCE and
join the Colours without delay:

(2) He can ATTEST AT ONCE UNDER
THE GROUP SYSTEM and be
called up in due course with his
Group.

If he does neither, a third course awaits him:
HE WILL BE DEEMED TO HAVE
ENLISTED
under the Military Service Act
ON THURSDAY, MARCH 2nd 1916.

HE WILL BE PLACED IN THE RESERVE.
AND BE CALLED UP IN HIS CLASS.
as the Military Authorities may determine.

A recruiting poster explaining the Military Service Act of 1916, the first occasion conscription was introduced into the British army.

either of the two main German surprises: huge howitzers and poison gas. Haig was much criticized for employing tanks while they were still in the experimental stage, but the Germans were very slow to bring anything similar into the field.

On 27 January 1916 the Military Service Act was passed; the long-revered principle of voluntary enlistment was abandoned in favour of conscription. In 1917 the huge conscripted citizen army of Great Britain, assisted by contingents from Canada, Australia, New Zealand, India and Newfoundland, fought the great battles of Messines, Passchendaele (Third Ypres) and Cambrai. The tanks at Cambrai achieved complete surprise initially, and penetrated nearly four miles behind the German front line, but the advance could not be sustained and all gains were wiped out by a tremendous German counter-attack. Yet these constant failures of the Allies were having the same effect on the German army as the oft-defeated Austrians had had on the armies of Napoleon. The enemy strength was draining away.

The huge German offensive opened on 21 March 1918. Its aim was to win the war with one last effort, and attacks were preceded by shattering barrages of high-explosive and gas shells which lasted only a few hours and were intended to disrupt rather than destroy. The Germans made advances so deep and alarming that on 9 April Haig issued his famous Order of the Day: 'With our backs to the wall and believing in the justice of our cause each one must fight on to the end.' On 18 July the French made a surprise tank attack in great strength from the forest of Villers-Cotterets and threw the Germans back. On 8 August Haig set in motion the Second Battle of the Somme, and 534 tanks broke the German front. The exhausted German army was never again able to recreate the old impregnable defence on ground of its own choosing and in a long series of victories the Allies, joined now by the Americans, drove the enemy back to the borders of Germany. The Armistice was signed against a background of mutiny in the German fleet and revolution in Germany, and all firing ceased at the eleventh hour of the eleventh day of the eleventh month in 1918.

Although France and the Western Front had been the main theatre of war, absorbing most of Britain's war effort and accounting for the great proportion of casualties – her involvement on the Italian front against the Austrians was in no way comparable – the need to protect the Suez Canal and the Persian oil-fields had led to major campaigns against the Turks in Mesopotamia and Palestine. Allenby's capture of Jerusalem, subsequent advance into Syria and defeat of the German commanders Falkenhayn and Liman von Sanders were long regarded as textbook examples of how such a campaign should be conducted. British naval power enabled British expeditions to capture German colonies, although in German East Africa (later known as Tanganyika and then Tanzania) General von Lettow-Vorbeck with only 3,500 Germans and 12,000 African *askari* kept a very much larger force of troops of the British Empire fully occupied until just after the Armistice.

Campaigns against the Turks, which did not affect the German war effort and did not draw any German troops away from the Western Front, kept about 1,500,000 Imperial troops away from the Western theatre, and since the final defeat of Turkey did no material damage to German power, it seems doubtful now whether much could in fact have been achieved if the Gallipoli campaign had succeeded.

However, at the end of the war Britain's greatest industrial and naval rival appeared to be completely destroyed and in the throes of internal revolution which threatened her survival as a European power. At the fearful cost of 745,000 dead Britain's regular, volunteer and conscripted army, allied with the fine troops of the Empire, had won the greatest victory in their history in what was claimed to be the 'War to End War'.

Chapter Six

THE CALM AND THE STORM

When the Great War was over, Britain as usual rewarded her soldiers by immediately dismantling the huge machine created to win it, and sending back into civilian life the great wealth of loyalty and talent which the citizen army had brought to every arm and department of the service. Since the government failed to impose on employers any obligation to give back to men returning from the army the jobs they had formerly held, many of those who had endured the hell of the trenches were unable to find any employment and were reduced to begging in the streets.

Rudyard Kipling had already done a great deal to flick the collective British conscience on the raw and remind complacent civilians how much they owed to the soldier:

> Yes, makin' mock o' uniforms that guard you while you sleep
> Is cheaper than them uniforms, an' they're starvation cheap.

And in his poem 'Tommy' he had emphasized how much the soldier was reviled in peace and fawned upon in war. But after this world war the problems of rehabilitation were not confined to a few thousand men but to millions. The very magnitude of the task seemed to discourage everyone from trying to do anything about it.

Naturally, after the slaughter in France, there was a revulsion from all things military which took the form of passionate pacifism, and the tide flowed strongly not just against war but against soldiers. Haig was accused of stupidity, callousness and incompetence. Yet the figure of dead which caused all this feeling was less than half that of the French losses and certainly not proportionately higher than that of previous wars against a major power. The trouble was that in the past the burden of casualties had fallen on two minority groups of society, the upper middle class which provided the officers, and the starving and desperate elements of the working class and Irish peasantry from which the soldiers came. For the first time the nation had been made to realize what it cost to have and defend a great

Opposite: desert and mountain warfare in the Middle East during the First World War. *Above:* British Lewis gun post at Duadar in the Suez Canal defences. *Below:* a British Vickers machine-gun position overlooking the River Struma, Salonika.

135

The town of Ypres in 1918 –
the material legacy of war.

Empire, and since the nation considered that the cost, now revealed in terms of human life, was unacceptable, some scapegoat had to be found. The blame and the responsibility were placed on the regular professional military commanders, and there was of course much on which all the anti-army sentiment could feed. On the first day of the Battle of the Somme Sir Henry Rawlinson's troops, weighed down with anything from 120 to 180 pounds of equipment, had been made to advance uphill in broad daylight, shoulder to shoulder in well-dressed ranks not more than 100 yards apart. These tactics of Frederick the Great had been a gift to German machine-gunners; and many accounts of this and similar 'errors' were published.

Once again the nation dissociated itself from the army, and the army reverted to its role of the 1890s, a sort of colonial police force, since it was actively discouraged from planning or training for any future war by Winston Churchill's proposal – the 'Ten Year Rule', accepted by the Cabinet – that the Services should base all their plans and requirements on the assumption that there would be no major war for at least ten years. The nation lost all interest in its defence in the period from 1918 until 1938 and, with customary parsimoniousness, inhibited all progress and experiment in weapons, equipment and organization. The old concept of soldiering returned: a career as an officer was suitable for gentlemen who liked an active sporting and social life; a career as a soldier provided relief for the destitute. Training consisted largely of drill, musketry, marching and digging. 'Manœuvres' occupied some two weeks in the year. Provided battalions were smart on parade, discipline good, the venereal disease rate in single figures, and 'The Flag' could be 'shown' adequately in all the corners of the Empire, few worried about professionalism.

One factor which had a crippling effect on any chance the army might have had for bringing its equipment up to date was the third armed service, the Royal Air Force, which took its share of the meagre allotment of defence funds. In addition, because of a firm but misplaced belief in the immense strategic value of the bomber, and a feeling that any future war could be won by air power alone, unsupported by ground operations, the building of a bomber force took priority over equipping the army. There was no agreement or direction over strategic or tactical doctrine and the general muddle was caused largely by the complete refusal, at all levels, even to contemplate another 'Western Front' situation, or to come to any decision on the possible nature of any future war. Britain would adopt the old maritime policy, defending herself, her communications and her Empire, and reducing the enemy by air bombardment and naval blockade. Thus the Royal Navy took priority after the bomber force, and the army had to make do with any money that was left.

Germany and Italy, under their dictators Adolf Hitler and Benito Mussolini, seized the chance which they were offered by General

Recruiting posters between the wars stressed travel, sport and 'job satisfaction'.

German troops enter the Rhineland in 1936.

Franco in the Spanish Civil War (1936–9) to test equipment and train troops and aircrews for the coming contest that they felt would give them the shared mastery of Europe. It was not until 1937 that Britain began to perceive the writing on the wall and set out on a programme of rearmament. Even then, British strategists, disillusioned by the failure of the League of Nations and its inability to prevent either Mussolini's conquest of Abyssinia or the German reoccupation of the Rhineland in 1936, could not decide where the real threat lay. In the Far East, Japan menaced Australia, New Zealand, Malaya, Singapore, Burma and Borneo. The Italians now lay across the Imperial life-line of the Mediterranean, the Suez Canal and the Red Sea. Germany, with all her talk of the day of reckoning for all she had suffered in the Great War, threatened the home country. The problem was vast and unique.

In 1937 Leslie Hore-Belisha, who gave his name to a traffic beacon, the design of a barrack block and the introduction of a system of promotion based on years of service and not dead men's shoes (the Belisha Majors), became Secretary of State for War. Largely because there was so great a conflict of opinion and so many different schools of thought among the senior professionals, he relied for military advice on Captain (retired) Liddell Hart (later Sir Basil Liddell Hart), undoubtedly the foremost military thinker and writer of the day. Liddell Hart had resigned from the army over vexed questions of mechanization and the employment of mobile armoured forces, and it is ironical that his theories on the principles and practice of mobile war, and the use of 'tactical' aircraft in close support of fast-moving armoured columns, were adopted by the German General

Hore-Belisha and the Army Council in November 1939.

Staff and ignored in his own country. Since leaving the army, Liddell Hart had become the Military Correspondent to *The Times*. His association with Hore-Belisha led to the mechanization of the British army and, as was only to be expected, aroused widespread antagonism and distrust.

By the time of the Munich Crisis in 1938 the country was still in no position to take on a German army which, from the coming into power of the Nazi régime in 1933, had expanded from the figure of 100,000 men allowed in the Versailles Treaty, to a force of 105 divisions, approximately 1,000,000 men. Six of these divisions were *Panzer* (tank), and ten motorized. Neville Chamberlain, who returned from Munich waving a piece of paper and calling out, 'Peace for our time!', had signed the pact with Hitler partly as a result of this sense of Britain's weakness. In return for Hitler's worthless assurances of goodwill Chamberlain had allowed Germany to acquire the excellent Czech army.

In September 1939, when Britain had to go to war because of the German invasion of Poland, the modernization of the army had not made anything like enough progress; for instance, although the cavalry had lost their horses, there were still only three armoured divisions, one in Egypt and two (one still awaiting its tanks) in England. In the previous three years France had declined from a position of strength in relation to the weakness of Germany, and

British weakness and German strength. *Left:* Neville Chamberlain, the appeaser, showing the London crowds a copy of the infamous Munich Agreement in 1938, and claiming it meant 'Peace for our time'. *Below:* Nazi rally at Nuremberg, September 1936.

while Germany grew stronger and more determined to fight, France slid rapidly in the opposite direction. By cherishing pacifist illusions in a hostile world both Britain and France, obviously influenced by their losses in the Great War, had thrown away all the advantages gained by their victory in 1918.

There was a great deal of difference between the beginning of the war in August 1914 and the mobilization of September 1939. In 1939 there was none of the 'astonishing completeness', the result of ten years' planning and preparation. In 1914 a force of four infantry and one cavalry divisions had crossed the Channel by M + 14 (two weeks after Mobilization Day). In 1939 Britain warned France that the B.E.F. of four infantry and one armoured divisions could not cross before M + 33. The armoured division never arrived, and the whole force bore witness to desperate last-minute efforts to get it ready in time. Not until the last few months before the outbreak of war was any attempt made to build up an expeditionary force in any more tangible form than a Mobilization Plan. In March 1939 it had been decided to double the strength of the Territorial Army, making a total of twenty-six divisions, and these, added to the six divisions of the regular army, raised the strength of the British army to thirty-two divisions. The Compulsory Training Act was passed in May, calling up 'militiamen', better known as 'reservists', for six months' training.

The politicians had chosen the worst possible moment to declare war. The field force was utterly inadequate for a global conflict, and the effects of long stagnation still permeated the staff and command structure and all schools of instruction. At a time when the Germans were preaching Liddell Hart's doctrine of speed, flexibility and the taking of risks, the British, having largely lost touch with professionalism, were wedded to caution. The vital questions of the composition and tactical deployment of armour were unresolved, and the British passion for compromise had resulted in the separation of 'army tank brigades' from 'armoured divisions'. The army tank brigade had the slow, heavy 'I' tank for close co-operation with infantry, and the armoured divisions were equipped with fast, lightly armoured 'cruiser' and light tanks. In battle, which called for a careful equation of armoured protection and gunpower, speed and reliability, these tanks were neither one thing nor the other, and not until 1943 was a satisfactory armoured vehicle evolved.

Ever since 1918 British military thinking had shied away from the prospect of another Western Front – though all the frightfulness of France and Flanders were in fact recreated in the Second World War by Germany and Russia on the Eastern Front. There was no Western Front to compare with the First World War, despite the Maginot Line and the initial positions taken up by the B.E.F., because the German *Blitzkrieg* (lightning war) in 1940 swept it away, tumbled Belgium and France into ruin and forced the British army to fall back to the coast and effect a naval evacuation from

Dunkirk, much as Napoleon and Soult had compelled Sir John Moore to run for Corunna. Yet, since the final objective of the Allies was the defeat of the main German army in the field, the Western Front (or Second Front, as it became known) had to be re-established. All the campaigns in North Africa, Sicily and Italy which followed Dunkirk were merely a prelude to the renewed fighting in France of 1944.

When the war began, the field formations available for active service amounted to four divisions earmarked for France, approximately six infantry divisions and one armoured division (not fully equipped or organized) in the area of the Middle East, one division and one brigade in India and two brigades in Malaya. In addition, there were garrison troops dotted around the world from Jamaica to Shanghai. It was little enough with which to oppose Hitler's 105 divisions and, in due course, Mussolini's much-vaunted 'six million bayonets'. Expansion was severely limited by the inability of British

The 2nd Bn. Royal Inniskilling Fusiliers disembarking from H.M.S. *Royal Sovereign* at Cherbourg in September 1939. There was none of the 'completeness' of August 1914.

One of many 'calls to arm'.

Oil burning on the sea at
Stansund, Norway, in the
spring of 1940.

industry to adjust rapidly to the demands of the armed forces and, as in the First World War, both France and Britain had to rely on help from America. Nevertheless the Cabinet decided that the army would consist of fifty-five divisions by September 1941. This figure was too ambitious and soon had to be reduced to thirty-six. In view of the years of neglect and the general lack of preparedness it is not surprising that the first two years of the war were clouded by a long succession of disasters.

Neville Chamberlain had practised appeasement at Munich in 1938 and he now cherished the illusion that if the B.E.F. in France took no offensive action it would not be attacked by the Germans. Meanwhile the economic and naval blockade of Germany would bring down the German dictator. Despite Britain's unredeemable pledge given to Poland and the declarations of war by Britain and France, the German *Blitzkrieg* overwhelmed Poland in less than three weeks.

In the spring of 1940 a small combined operation to assist the Norwegians, who had been attacked in order to secure the ice-free port of Narvik for the passage of Swedish iron ore to the German war machine, ended in a failure which brought down Chamberlain's government. Winston Churchill, at the head of a coalition government, took over the responsibility for running the war.

The fighting in western Europe really began on 10 May 1940 when the *Blitzkrieg* was launched against the 'Western Front'. British

commanders had not appreciated the lessons of Poland and Norway and were still expecting an offensive on the lines of those in the Great War. Tanks, guns and screaming dive-bombers smashed their way through all Allied resistance, but a local counter-attack by the British 1st Army Tank Brigade at Arras halted the 7th Panzer Division, giving it a shock all the more unpleasant for being unexpected. This was a brief indication of the contribution Britain might have made had she rearmed earlier, and it influenced the decision by the German army commander von Rundstedt to halt the *Panzer* drive on Dunkirk. It was thus possible to evacuate 338,000 Allied troops (nearly 140,000 of them being French) from the beaches of Dunkirk in Operation DYNAMO. Disintegration of the French army followed swiftly and on 21 June 1940 France signed an armistice with Germany. Reminiscent of Napoleon on the raft in the River Niemen at Tilsit, Adolf Hitler had reached the peak of his career.

It was at this point that Mussolini entered the war and became, in Churchill's words, 'Hitler's Italian lackey'.

Britain now stood alone, facing the threat of a German invasion. To meet it she had a force of fifteen divisions, most of which had no transport and were desperately short of equipment.

The German invasion, Operation SEALION, never took place because Hitler's *Luftwaffe* (air force) failed to win air superiority and the Royal Navy guarded the Channel. The Battle of Britain, won

The beach at Dunkirk, 1940. Allied troops await evacuation by the 'little ships' that saved the survivors of the British Expeditionary Force.

by a handful of exhausted pilots, was the first significant set-back in the German dictator's dreams of everlasting conquest. Furthermore it gave Britain a little more badly needed time to mobilize her resources. Having now no Western Front in Europe, and faced with the same problem as that which Pitt the Younger and his successors had tried to solve after Napoleon had abandoned his plans for invasion, Churchill had no alternative to the maritime policy. The Combined Operations Command was set up and special assault troops, the commandos, were trained for raids on the coast of Europe. New regiments and corps came into being – the Army Air Corps, consisting of the Parachute Regiment, the Glider Pilot Regiment and the Special Air Service, and the Reconnaissance Corps.

Lacking an opportunity to attack the Germans, Britain turned her attention to the Italian empire: Libya, where Marshal Graziani commanded an army of 200,000 and, far away to the south-east, Abyssinia and Eritrea where garrison troops totalling another 200,000 threatened the main British source of oil in the Persian Gulf. In December 1940, 36,000 men of the Western Desert Force under General O'Connor attacked Graziani, and in a campaign lasting two months completely annihilated his army and opened the whole of Libya to occupation. Meanwhile another Allied force came up from Kenya through Italian Somaliland to Abyssinia. The 4th Indian Division, originally part of O'Connor's victorious army, took Eritrea after fierce fighting against unusually determined Italian troops at Keren, and by 17 May 1941 the Italian empire in East Africa no longer existed. Though all this was immensely cheering to the British who were becoming almost conditioned to disaster, it had no effect on the principal enemy, and the problem of creating an operational front against the Germans still remained.

Mussolini's invasion of Greece in December 1940, launched from Italian-owned Albania, seemed to offer an opportunity in the Balkans, because instead of gaining a victory as easy as their invasion of Abyssinia in 1936, the Italians were thrown out by the Greeks who then counter-invaded Albania. Hitler, busy with plans to invade Russia, was irritated by Mussolini's failure – he had not been informed that the operation was to take place – and because he wanted to avoid trouble on his right flank when his armies poured into Russia, he decided to mount a German counter-counter-invasion, destroy all Greek resistance and the small British ground and air forces which had gone to strengthen it. News of this intention reached Churchill and, unfortunately, as it turned out, the decision was taken to break up General O'Connor's army and send an expeditionary force to Greece in the hope that the Yugoslavs and Turks might come in on the side of the Allies.

The Yugoslavs collapsed almost at once under the impact of five German divisions. The Turks remained neutral. Five other German divisions, three of them armoured, compelled the 6th Australian

Division, the 1st New Zealand Division and one British armoured brigade to withdraw and re-embark with the loss of their heavy equipment which, at this stage, could not be spared. The campaign had been more or less a repetition of what had happened in France, and the British and Imperial troops had again been swept away by the speed and power of the highly organized *Blitzkrieg*, supported by 800 aircraft. Against this armada the 80 available aircraft of the Royal Air Force could do little. But the expeditionary force did not retreat tamely. It fought with the ferocious tenacity for which the Australians and New Zealanders in particular are famous.

The evacuation of Crete, June 1941.

In May 1941 the Germans delivered an overwhelming airborne attack on the British and Imperial forces in Crete, and the very scale of the assault should have been immediately decisive. But the resistance offered by the hopelessly outnumbered garrison was so savage that in a fortnight, although compelled to withdraw, the British and Imperial forces inflicted losses on the German airborne formations from which they never really recovered.

The main result of failing to complete the occupation of Libya, breaking up O'Connor's army and sending the expedition to Greece was that Hitler was able to intervene in North Africa. He sent two *Panzer* divisions, in what became known as the *Afrika Korps* under the command of Lieutenant-General Erwin Rommel, to rescue the

Chivalrous opponents:
Field-Marshals Auchinleck
(*left*), and Rommel (*right*).

Italian colony. In Rommel's first attack, seven days before the
Germans entered Yugoslavia, the weak garrison that had replaced
O'Connor's Australian, New Zealand and Indian divisions was
outmanœuvred and captured. For the next two years the campaigns
in the Western Desert, fought, in the main, along the old-fashioned
lines of British sportsmanship and German chivalry, dominated
Press, radio and newsreels to the exclusion of the far more important
and far more arduous and difficult campaigns against the Japanese
in the Far East. It became an obsession with Churchill that Rommel,
whose *Afrika Korps* seldom numbered more than 50,000 men,
should be defeated and driven out of Africa.

In November 1941 General Sir Claude Auchinleck ('The Auk')
and the newly constituted British Eighth Army began Operation
CRUSADER. Rommel was driven back to the borders of Tripoli-
tania, over the ground taken by General O'Connor a year before,
and while this battle was being fought the Japanese attacked the
American fleet, lying at Pearl Harbor in the Hawaiian group of
islands in the Pacific, on 7 December. Borneo and Malaya came
under Japanese attack, and the strategic nightmare that had haunted
British planners at the time of rearmament before the war had now
become reality.

Although the total strength of the British army in December 1941
was nearly 2,500,000 men, the deployment of them, set against the

over-all defence of the Empire, was out of balance. The main weight
was in the Middle East. Now, just at the moment when Auchinleck
was in position to strike through to Tripoli, he had to send men and
equipment to Malaya and Burma.

Shortage of equipment, especially tanks; an attitude of *laissez-
faire* between the wars; a reluctance on the part of the authorities in
the Far East to appreciate the seriousness of the Japanese threat and,
above all, an inability to cope with the tactics of enemy formations
advancing swiftly on bicycles along jungle roads and tracks – all
these combined to enable the Japanese to drive all before them. On
15 February 1942 Singapore surrendered to them, with the loss of
70,000 men, most of whom were recently arrived reinforcements in
no condition after a long voyage to fight this kind of war. General
Harold Alexander gathered up all the troops he could find in Burma,
conducted a masterly retreat through the whole length of the
country, and led them across the mountains into India.

Up to now, in India, there had been very little change in the
peaceful, well-ordered life of garrison troops who had not been
required for operations on the North-West Frontier or as reinforcements for the Middle East. India had been regarded as a base, a
source of manpower and a factory for war material. Now, with the
Japanese swarming up into the Manipur Hills, she was in the front
line.

Yet the Japanese, like the Germans carrying out the Schlieffen
Plan in 1914, had overreached themselves. They needed time to
mount their invasion of India. The British Fourteenth Army held

Perhaps the darkest moment
in all British military history,
the surrender of the British
to the Japanese at Singapore
on 15 February 1942.

Prime Minister and war-leader Winston Churchill viewing the Alamein defensive position on 7 August 1942, while Auchinleck was still in command.

them in stalemate along the Burmese frontier until 1944, while the counter-attack that was to drive them out of Burma was being prepared.

During this time the men of the Eighth Army in the Middle East continued the contest against Rommel, largely unaware that they had certain considerable disadvantages. Rommel's troops had developed the theory of the battle group, a mixed force of tanks, self-propelled artillery and lorried infantry which, because the Germans had no rigid divisional or brigade formation, could be formed, augmented or thinned even while a battle was being fought. This gave the *Afrika Korps* a flexibility that was entirely lacking in its opponents. The British armour consisted mainly of the great cavalry regiments whose forebears had broken the *Grande Armée* at Waterloo and charged the guns at Balaclava, and tended to fight battles on their own, 'giving', as *Punch* once put it, 'a little tone to what would otherwise be a vulgar brawl'. The large infantry

German troops on the move in the Western Desert, North Africa.

General Sir Bernard
Montgomery watching the
Alamein attack from the
turret of a Grant tank in
October 1942.

divisions had their own problems of mobility in the desert. Anti-tank
guns were used mainly in defence. The whole staff system was rigid
and cumbersome. Even though they were operating in the vast open
spaces of the desert where the north coast was the only recognizable
flank, commanders were still thinking in terms of set-piece attack,
defence and withdrawal, a mechanized repetition of the Flanders
battles of the First World War. The Royal Air Force was an entirely
separate Service, with its own job to do.

In the summer of 1942, from the last week in May until the end of
June, Rommel attacked his unco-ordinated enemies, captured
Tobruk and 30,000 prisoners of war, utterly defeated the Eighth
Army and pushed what was left of it right back into Egypt. General
Auchinleck, Commander-in-Chief in the Middle East, took over
personal command of the demoralized army. At the First Battle of
Alamein he directed his main effort at Rommel's Italian troops, took
the initiative, threw Rommel back and saved Egypt. His attempt
to exploit this success at the end of July did not succeed mainly
because he lacked the strength, and also because of the limitations
imposed by poor co-operation between armour and infantry. His
decision to overcome this problem by creating mixed divisions
containing a balanced force of tanks, infantry and guns on the
pattern of the *Afrika Korps* was not implemented because Churchill
dismissed him. General Alexander became Commander-in-Chief
and Montgomery took over the Eighth Army.

At the end of August Rommel attacked again, aiming for Suez,
and was thoroughly defeated in the Battle of Alam Halfa, Montgomery's carefully planned defensive battle. On 23 October,
Montgomery took the offensive and fought the Second Battle of
Alamein which, except in losses and outcome, had much in common
with the Battle of the Somme in 1916. There were no flanks. Rommel

lay in a strong, immensely deep defensive position with his right resting on the impassable soft sand of the Quattara Depression and his left on the sea. There was no alternative to a frontal attack against positions softened up by massive, though brief, ground and air bombardment, and a hard slogging fight to break through into the open country beyond. The initial momentum was lost because infantry and armour still could not work properly together, and the battle lasted for twelve days. Enormous numbers of Italian prisoners were taken. Rommel conducted a brilliant retreat over 1,500 miles and the British pursuit was a triumph of administration.

Four days after Rommel's withdrawal from Alamein an Anglo-American force made an assault landing in great strength along the coasts of Morocco and Algeria. The entry of Americans into the war, after Pearl Harbor, with their immense reservoirs of men and material, changed the whole course of the war. Britain had exhausted all her economic resources by the end of 1941; without unstinted American help under the Lend-Lease Acts she would not have been able to continue the struggle. Ever since King William's War she had been able to hire mercenaries and pay poorer nations to fight for her. She now found herself the subsidized ally of a greater power which, because it was now taking an active part in the fighting, was able to call the tune.

Alamein was the last offensive against German and Italian troops conducted by the British alone – with their Imperial troops. It was

Rifles being unloaded in England: part of a lend-lease shipment from the U.S.A.

undoubtedly a turning-point in the war, but more from a morale point of view than anything else.

All Axis resistance in North Africa ended in May 1943. The way to Sicily and Italy lay open. The fall of Sicily led to the surrender of Italy and the ruin of Mussolini. There seemed to be a chance that the Italian peninsula might serve the same purpose as the Iberian peninsula in the war against Napoleon: a theatre in which a small British force could tap and drain away the enemy's strength at little cost. But the Germans, who fought on in Italy, had short and excellent lines of communication back to Germany whereas those of the Allies ran back across the Mediterranean and thence to England or America by way of Gibraltar. The terrain of Italy, with its mountainous spine, deep valleys and broad rivers, gave full scope to the ingenuity of the Germans in defence, and the seaborne operations to turn successive positions – at Salerno in 1943 for example, and Anzio in 1944 – were pinned down initially in narrow beach-heads by the swiftness of German reaction to any new threat. The road to Rome was long and bloody and the city cost the Eighth Army nine months of battle. The brief pursuit was afterwards halted by the Gothic Line which ran from Pisa in the west to Rimini in the

Allied Planning Conference in North Africa, 1943. From left to right around Churchill: Foreign Secretary Eden, General Brooke, Air Chief Marshal Tedder, Admiral Cunningham, Generals Alexander, Marshall (U.S.A.), Eisenhower (U.S.A.) and Montgomery.

Costly assaults on Fortress Europe. The Italian Campaign, 1944: British troops at Monte Cassino, which held out for three months.

east; it was penetrated at last in September 1944 after a long series of costly frontal assaults. Even then, the war in Italy was not over, and not until the general collapse of the German armies in the spring of 1945 was it possible for the Allies to break through the final positions.

It had long been accepted by the Allies that Germany could not be broken until a 'Second Front' – counterpart to the Russian Front – had been established in northern France, but the problems of invasion had been highlighted by the disastrous raid on Dieppe in July 1942. This made it clear that there could be little hope of capturing a fortified port (all ports were fortified after the Dieppe raid); yet without a fully operational major port it would not be possible to maintain a force of the size needed to break through the Atlantic Wall – the German name for their coastal defence system. Any assault would have to be made over open beaches after crossing a stretch of water which, from the point of view of weather, is the most unpredictable and unreliable in the world. The problem of initial supply was solved by brilliant British inventors who designed the floating harbours, given the code name MULBERRY, which completely upset all the German intelligence forecasts.

The date and time factors for the invasion were critical because of the unprecedented scale of the operation, the nature of the deception which led the Germans to believe, until it was too late, that the assault

The Dieppe disaster, August 1942: abandoned British landing craft and 'amphibious' tanks.

would come in the Pas de Calais, and the need to achieve surprise. In fact, strategic and tactical surprise were complete because when the Allies came ashore they did so on a line between the River Orne and the Cotentin peninsula, in bad weather, at high tide and at the time of the full moon, a combination considered by the Germans to create impossible conditions. By the evening of D-Day, 6 June 1944, the Allies had established a firm beach-head.

The German response was rapid and vigorous, and there was bitter fighting in the Caen area before the situation reached the point where the American armour could break out in the southern sector, pour west across Brittany and then along the line of the River Loire to Paris. The German army, weakened by the relentless onslaught of the Russians along the Eastern Front, was not of the same standard as Rommel's *Afrika Korps*.

In the middle of August 1944, after fierce battles round Falaise, the German defenders of France withdrew towards the Fatherland. But the resilience of Hitler's *Wehrmacht* was astonishing: by the autumn the Allies had been checked on a line running south from the North Sea, across Holland, through Aachen to the Alps. The gallant attempt by the British 1st Airborne Division to break through only just failed at Arnhem, and in December, against all the odds, Field-Marshal von Rundstedt counter-attacked in the Ardennes, in what became known as the 'Battle of the Bulge'. It was the last desperate

The Normandy triumph –
the D-Day landings, June
1944.

The preliminary
bombardment before the
crossing of the Rhine in
March 1945, the greatest
artillery barrage of the war.

German gamble. The thrust was contained and then beaten back. In
March, British and Canadian troops of 21st Army Group crossed the
Rhine north of the industrial area of the Ruhr, and the Americans
crossed to the south. The British drove north towards Lübeck and
the Baltic; the Americans went east to meet the Russians and south
through Bavaria. The Russian tide flowed irresistibly westwards.
On 5 May 1945 Field-Marshal Montgomery accepted the un-
conditional surrender of all German land, sea and air forces in
Holland, Denmark and north-west Germany. The war in the west
was over; the war against the Japanese went on.

The magnificent exploits of Britain's Fourteenth Army, in
perhaps the worst conditions that any Allied force had to contend
with, were so often driven out of the newspapers by events nearer
home that the troops called themselves the 'Forgotten Army'. In a
campaign lasting from March until July 1944 this forgotten army
fought the battles of Kohima and Imphal, and not only saved India
but destroyed the Japanese force on the frontier. In ferocious hand-
to-hand fighting from trenches sometimes no further apart than the
length of a district commissioner's tennis court (at Kohima), the
Japanese as usual showed a complete disregard for death and an
ability to exist, and fight, apparently without food and water, for
days on end. Air superiority and air supply were the crucial factors.
The Royal Air Force swept the skies clean of Japanese aircraft while
their Dakotas dropped ammunition, food and medical supplies to

Opposite above: Field-
Marshal Montgomery
(centre right) accepts the
German surrender on the
Western Front from Rear-
Admiral Wagner (far left)
and Admiral von Friedberg
(centre left), 5 May 1945.

Opposite below: the Burma
Campaign: loading engineer
stores at a Field Park during
the monsoon, Kohima 1944.

isolated pockets of British and Imperial troops on the ground. On 8 July 1944 the Japanese broke and fell back into Burma along a route lined with the stinking corpses of men who had died of wounds, starvation and disease. This great victory was obscured in England by what was happening in Normandy.

The reconquest of Burma by General Sir William (later Field-Marshal Lord) Slim and the Fourteenth Army was certainly one of the most difficult and brilliant offensive campaigns in the whole history of the British army. It was fought through densely forested valleys and mountains, across great rivers such as the Chindwin, Irrawaddy and Sittang. The lines of communication from India, with all the necessary roads, bridges and airfields, had to be built. River-crossing craft had to be constructed as the need arose. Troops had to contend with tropical diseases, leeches and all the discomforts of the Burmese jungle.

In March 1945 the fate of the 'Armies of the Rising Sun' was sealed when Slim completely deceived the Japanese, took his army across the Irrawaddy and recaptured Mandalay and Meiktila. The Japanese evacuated Rangoon, already heavily bombed by American Liberator aircraft from India, and retreated into the 'Moulmein Box'. Here they were systematically destroyed. The Burma campaign was over by 6 May 1945; an event completely eclipsed by the surrender of Germany.

Operation ZIPPER, the plan for the reconquest of Malaya and Singapore, was about to begin when the Japanese surrendered. They had been utterly defeated by the United States in the long series of combined operations ending in the capture of the island of Okinawa, and the dropping of the atomic bombs on Hiroshima and Nagasaki in August 1945.

Thus, at the very end of the greatest war in history, there appeared a weapon with powers of destruction and devastation so appalling that it not only seemed to close the chapter of 'conventional' gunpowder wars but made out of date most of the accepted principles and criteria on which such wars had been based.

The reconquest of Burma in 1945 by the 'Forgotten Army' under General (later Field-Marshal Lord) Slim (*above*) was one of the toughest and most brilliant campaigns in the history of the army. Locally built river-crossing equipment had to be used, such as that shown (*opposite above*) being unloaded in the jungle at Myitson (February 1945). The Japanese were dogged opponents: snipers had to be cleared one by one from these pagodas on Mandalay Hill (*opposite below*).

Chapter Seven

THE DISSOLUTION OF EMPIRE

In the years just before the Second World War there had been several different schools of thought on the question of 'decisive' factors in war. Chamberlain, like the younger Pitt before him, had believed in causing economic collapse. Liddell Hart had laid much emphasis on the tank. Many people were convinced, and despite all the evidence went on being convinced, that aerial bombardment alone could produce a result. It was unfortunate that no one had really interpreted the true message of the Guernica attack in the Spanish Civil War. The deliberate and prolonged bombing of this little undefended town on market day, 27 April 1937, as an exercise in terror by the German Condor Legion, killed and wounded 2,600 civilians and terrified a great many more, but the effect of it was to stiffen the corporate will to resist. The massive 'pattern' bombing of German civilians by the Allied air forces had a similar result.

It is the army which in the end wins wars. No enemy is really defeated until infantry with rifles and bayonets take possession of his towns and patrol the countryside. The two atomic explosions in

Opposite: the ultimate weapon of the Second World War; the atomic bomb explodes at Hiroshima, August 1945.

On the Road to Mandalay. It is the army which in the end wins wars, and has to maintain personal contact with the local population.

Fitting out recruits in the First World War.

1945 affected the people of Japan profoundly, but they did not really appreciate the extent of their defeat until American soldiers were seen in the streets. While the balance of nuclear power remains comparatively even between East and West the 'Bomb' may well be an effective deterrent to global war, simply because it appears obvious that a nuclear holocaust will decide nothing. In the meantime it is the soldier with his conventional weapons, supported by armour, artillery and tactical aircraft, who is the symbol of military power.

Britain's army had always been extremely small by comparison with the enormous conscript armies of the Continent. It had been split up in countless little garrisons and detachments all over the world and the administrative problems had been proportionately small. But by the summer of 1916 Haig's field force in France consisted of sixty-two divisions grouped in five armies. More than 2,000,000 men had to be provided with all the normal requirements of everyday life as well as medical cover, clothing, ammunition, transport, communications and 'welfare' in the form of off-duty recreation. In the past the administration of troops in the field had been a traditional failing in the British army, but this time it was raised to a standard never reached before.

The Army Service Corps handled all supplies and transport and expanded to ten times its pre-war size. A system of issuing pay through field cashiers and base cashiers was evolved; the Medical Services rose from a figure of 200 to nearly 11,000 officers, and from 500 up to 6,000 nursing staff; the workshops of the Ordnance Corps grew into large factories. The Army Postal Service had to handle 10,000,000 letters a week, and in 1916 the Expeditionary Force Canteen Service came into being. The whole vast administrative

organization, on a scale never even contemplated previously and yet set up within two years, worked with extraordinary efficiency and met all the demands made on it. It was a far cry from the Crimean War, when troops starved while two miles away large quantities of food were rotting on the ships in Balaclava Harbour.

Fortunately the principles and general systems on which the administrative services of the First World War had been based were preserved. Even the teaching at the Royal Military College Sandhurst between the wars included such subjects as medical evacuation from front-line units to base hospitals, 'The Corps System of Ammunition Supply', and so on, so that when the time came, expansion was a routine matter. Yet the administrative problems of the static war in

Food supply in the First World War. *Above:* an Expeditionary Service mobile canteen on the Italian Front, 1918. *Left:* the static conditions on the Western Front allowed this disused communication trench on Vimy Ridge to be used as a vegetable patch (1918).

Air Supply; the R.A.F. drops supplies to West African troops in the Arakan, Burma, in November 1944.

France had been simple and straightforward by comparison with the ones that arose in the Second World War. The ports of Calais, Boulogne, Dieppe and Le Havre, only a matter of a few hours from England, had all been available to Haig's staff. In the war which began in 1939 there were separate theatres in the Middle East, East Africa, Burma, Sicily, Italy and north-west Europe. All had their own special problems, and periods of comparative immobility alternated with intense activity over huge distances. The administrative services in each theatre of war were stretched almost to the limit; but the limit was never reached and the services lived up magnificently to the slogan pinned in many an office and tent: 'The impossible we do at once. Miracles may take a few minutes longer.'

Air supply was developed far beyond all previous calculations. The defeat of the Japanese and the reconquest of Burma would have been impossible without it. Very nearly all (96 per cent) of the Fourteenth Army's supplies were delivered by air – more than 500,000 tons. The whole concept of administration, based on the static conditions of the First World War, had had to be reconsidered after what happened in Norway and France in 1940. The communications system, in which wireless served only to bridge a gap when landlines were cut by enemy shelling, could not function in mobile operations. Long-distance radio became essential but problems of design, development and manufacture delayed the delivery of reliable sets

Communications. In the First World War the despatch rider (*below*) was pre-eminent – here one is helped by a German prisoner to push his motorcycle through the mud of what was once Mametz Wood (July 1916). Long-distance radio was essential for the more mobile operations of the Second World War: landlines, shown (*left*) being checked in Burma, were liable to be cut by enemy shelling.

in adequate numbers until 1944. The days of the messenger on a horse and the runner stumbling through shell craters had gone for ever; radio waves became the very pulse of the army, and the first Director of Signals was appointed in 1941. The size, scope and operational commitments of the Corps of Royal Engineers expanded enormously, particularly in the field of civil engineering. Engineers had to build roads, railways, airfields and pipelines. They had to operate ports, railway systems and inland waterways. They became assault troops, moving forward in their own armoured vehicles to destroy enemy minefields and defence works, and to bridge obstacles for the tanks coming up behind them. In 1941 an Engineer-in-Chief was appointed as the engineer adviser to the Chief of the Imperial General Staff on all engineer matters concerning policy and operations.

The Royal Army Service Corps, which has since (in 1967) become the Royal Corps of Transport, ran its own small merchant marine service. It maintained supplies by road, rail, air and water to troops operating in conditions which varied from the heat of the North African desert in July to the monsoon downpour in the Kabaw Valley in Burma. It was so consistently and superbly efficient that it was taken for granted. The Royal Army Ordnance Corps, previously geared to a system of issue and collection through static field parks and depots, smoothly adapted itself to the requirements of mobile operations in a global war, providing clothing and ammunition and other stores on an unprecedented scale, operating bath units and laundries, and developing its own factories in occupied enemy territory.

Military engineering: bridge-building in Burma in the Second World War.

Military engineering:
building a light railway in
the wake of the British
advance during the Battle of
Messines in 1917.

The vast increase in the number of vehicles issued by Ordnance
to the rest of the army and the great advances in the technology of
weapons and equipment led to the formation of the Royal Corps of
Electrical and Mechanical Engineers in October 1942. The new
Corps was responsible for the maintenance and repair of all electrical
and mechanical equipment, from a prismatic compass to an armoured
self-propelled gun. The repair organization consisted of four
'echelons': Light Aid Detachments with forward units, mobile
workshops on a brigade basis, heavy equipment workshops further
back and base workshops which were complete factories.

Though the task of the Royal Army Medical Corps had not
changed it was greatly affected by the advances in medicine and
surgery and by the mobility of warfare. The old system of casualty
treatment and evacuation, adequate in static warfare, was brought
up to date with a far more flexible organization which made good
use of aircraft. The effort devoted to the soldier's welfare was far
greater than it had been in the previous war. The old Army Canteen
Service and regimental canteens and institutes were replaced by the
Navy, Army and Air Force Institute (NAAFI) which provided
everything from a combined club room, bar, restaurant and shop
in a unit, to leave camps and Service Clubs of a very high standard.

In the 'teeth arms' the differences between cavalry and infantry,
and the tactical independence which this had caused, were overcome by re-designing the organization of a division, in 1942, to
create a balanced fighting force of all arms. The armoured division
now consisted of a brigade (three regiments) of tanks, a lorried
infantry brigade (three battalions), an armoured car regiment and
organic artillery, engineers and signals. This was further developed
in the form of the independent armoured brigade which had three
armoured regiments, one infantry battalion in trucks, and its own

gunners and sappers. It was the reorganization originally proposed by General Auchinleck in the Western Desert, and the forerunner of the modern battle group. The principal result of this integrated organization of Horse, Foot and Guns was a spirit of co-operation and a sense of team-work within the army which had seldom existed before.

The personal weapon in the infantry was still the Lee-Enfield rifle, but by the end of the war light machine-guns, two-inch and three-inch mortars and anti-tank weapons gave formidable fire power to a battalion. The anti-tank weapons were 17-pounder guns and Projectors Infantry Anti-Tank, the PIAT. The latter was fired from the shoulder and launched a high-explosive armour-piercing missile resembling a mortar bomb on a flat trajectory. For a time the predominance of the rifle was threatened by the machine-carbine, first the Thompson .45 inch made in America, and then the Sten. The Sten, which fired a nine millimetre calibre round, was an unsophisticated weapon, cheap and easy to make (9,000,000 were produced during the war), but it was essentially a close-range weapon and, because of its comparatively high cyclic rate of fire, like all automatic weapons it created its own problems of ammunition supply.

The soldier of the Second World War differed considerably from his counterpart in the war of 1914–18. The 'Old Contemptible' and his immediate successors in Kitchener's Army and the later conscript

Medical Services: a horse ambulance standing outside a Regimental Aid Post during the Battle of the Menin Road in 1917.

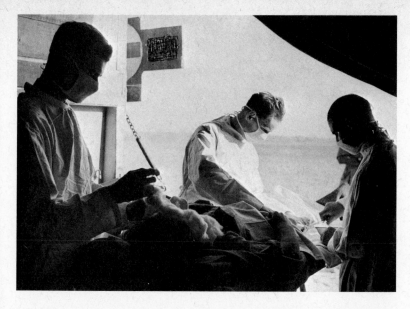

force were products of the Victorian and Edwardian age of discipline.
Their unquestioning obedience stemmed mainly from a low standard
of education, a considerable ignorance of anything outside the
small circle of their lives, and a general acceptance of life as it was.
There was no Welfare State then, to look after the man who lost his
job. Life was cheap, wages were low and unemployment a constant
threat. People became accustomed to doing what they were told.
Stoicism was a national characteristic, and indeed for centuries it
had been the principal attribute of the ordinary soldier in the ranks.

The soldier of the 1939–45 war was better educated and his
horizon had been extended by the cinema, the radio, newspapers
and magazines. Unlike the majority of his predecessors he came into
the army as a conscript, not as a volunteer, and he tended to bring
with him a slight undertone of resentment and accusation. The so-
called 'ruling classes' had failed to solve the problems facing the
country between the wars, and now he had been called up to fight a
war they should have prevented. Most conscripts accepted the
situation; nevertheless there were many whose attitude to authority
was by no means one of blind obedience. Officers soon learned how
much depended on proper leadership and man-management, and
the senior commanders went to considerable lengths to ensure that
they personally and their plans were known to the men they sent
into battle. It was a new kind of leadership and a new kind of
relationship.

Even so, the characteristics of the British soldier as a fighting man
were much as they had always been. He was incapable of developing
the single-minded concentration of, for example, the German, on
the task of defeating the enemy. He could not be persuaded to take
war seriously. 'The British soldier must be driven to digging himself

Trouble in India; a lone British soldier guards the Calcutta Market, burned and looted after rioting between Hindus and Muslims (1946).

in the moment he occupies an area,' wrote the commander of the 56th Division in the Arakan (Burma) in 1944, 'and not to waste time in sight-seeing, souvenir hunting and brewing tea.' When necessary he fought with the dogged determination and unflinching courage of his ancestors, then he would roll over on his back, light a cigarette and wait to be told what to do next. Always reluctant to take advantage of a defeated enemy, he could rarely be persuaded to pursue with vigour. Marlborough and Wellington had had just the same trouble.

At the end of the Second World War Britain still had large armies, intact and victorious; but she was in fact in the same position as France after the wars of Louis XIV: exhausted and ruined. She could no longer afford to maintain her great Empire. All the wealth and power and possessions gained since the last decade of the seventeenth century had flowed away down the channel cut for her own survival. A whole volume of British history had come to an end; the next one was just beginning.

The first sacrifice shattered the entire framework of the Empire. Hitherto, India had been the focal point of all Imperial strategy. The main lines of communication – Gibraltar, Malta, Cyprus, Egypt and Aden; South Africa, Dar es Salaam, Mombasa, the Seychelles and Ceylon; Hong Kong, Borneo, Malaya, Singapore and Rangoon – had all led to India. For generations, service in India, internal security duties in the garrisons of the plains and mountain warfare in the hills of the North-West Frontier, had been part of the life of practically every soldier. And to those who can look back on it, it was the best part. In 1947 a Labour government gave independence to the subcontinent, divided into India and Pakistan. When the veil of sentiment and illusion is drawn aside it can be seen that there was no

alternative. It was a painfully realistic decision based on the poverty of Britain and the hostility of Indian politicians. India could not be held by force. British troops prepared to leave. The Indian politicians claimed a great victory, but the soldiers who had served India as well if not better than their own country, marched to the docks through silent crowds and many wept to see them go. The tears were justified. When the British army, which, in the words of Sir John Fortescue, 'will be remembered best not for its countless deeds of daring and invincible stubbornness in battle, but for its lenience in conquest and its gentleness in domination', left its garrisons, the communities in which peace had been so carefully preserved burst into an inferno of slaughter.

Soon, very little remained of the great Indian Empire. Ceylon became a dominion, Burma preferred to be an independent country outside the Commonwealth. Malaya and Borneo were high on the list of countries which were to govern themselves. Suddenly the whole purpose of the lines of communication ceased to exist. The routes through the Mediterranean and round the Cape of Good Hope led nowhere, and it would have been only a matter of common sense to withdraw from Egypt, Palestine, Libya, Malta, Cyprus and Aden, all of which required large garrisons and contained expensive installations; but the Conservative government which came into power in 1951 would not endorse the policy of the Labour Prime Minister Attlee and rid the country of the 'shackles of Empire'.

In the meantime, while politicians wavered, in many countries the 'spirit of nationalism and hunger for independence' sparked off violent demonstrations. With little warning, British officers and their soldiers found themselves trying to keep the peace in countries to whose former friendly inhabitants they were now enemies. They had to deal with riots and terrorism, with snipers and gunmen who

173

Trouble in Palestine; a soldier of the Highland Light Infantry covers a Jerusalem street with his Bren gun, to the total unconcern of Arab women and their donkeys (1947).

refused to fight in the open. Britain could not stand long against the tide now flowing against her.

In 1948 the garrison of Palestine was withdrawn and the Arab-Israeli conflict began. A new Middle East base was built at great expense at Fayid in the Canal Zone and the garrison of Egypt was concentrated there. This too was abandoned in the face of Egyptian terrorism in 1954. The base was divided between Kenya and Cyprus. Kenya was the 'spring-board', so the politicians said, for the Far East. But the Indian Empire was no more. The first faint rumbles of trouble coming in Kenya were heard in 1947, when the King's African Rifles had to deal with labour riots in Mombasa. In 1953 the situation became serious when the Mau-Mau movement set out to 'free Kenya from the imperialist yoke'. After order had been restored, Kenya and the new base built at Mackinnon Road, were handed over to the political leaders who had instigated the Mau-Mau Rebellion.

In Cyprus an 'emergency' began in April 1955. The Greek Cypriots, who seemed unable to make up their minds between fighting the British for their 'freedom' and among themselves for union with Greece, specialized in shooting unarmed servicemen and their wives in the back, usually while they were out shopping. Cyprus, under the political Archbishop, Makarios, gained her independence but the vexed questions of *Enosis*, union with Greece, is still a live issue, as has been made clear by the attempted Greek Cypriot *coup* and subsequent Turkish invasion of the island in July 1974.

During this time, while the British soldier was acting as a target and the scapegoat for all the trouble in the Middle East and East

Africa, he was also fighting Communism in the forests and rubber plantations of Malaya. The battle for Malaya lasted from 1948 until 1960 and ended in the first, and so far only, total success gained by any Western power over Chinese-trained guerrilla forces putting into effect the theories of revolutionary warfare expounded by the Chinese Communist leader Mao Tse-tung. This was part of the 'Cold War', the ideological conflict between Communism and Western ideas of democracy which had started even before the end of the Second World War. In 1945 British troops had been involved in 'incidents' on the borders of Communist Yugoslavia, and had supported the Greek government in a bitter war against Communist guerrillas in 1946 and 1947.

Events in Yugoslavia and Greece made the Allies realize that their forces acting as armies of occupation in the countries of their former enemies now had the primary role of defending the West against Communist aggression from the East, but, by 1948, although the Russian military capability had not diminished at all, demobilization had dissipated the immense Allied strength. It would now have to be rebuilt.

The first step in the reconstruction process was the creation of the Western Union organization, formed by the Treaty of Brussels signed in March 1948, and for the first time in her history Britain committed herself to providing a force which would be stationed on the Continent in peacetime. Her willingness to become involved in any future continental war was prompted by the Russian *coup d'état* in Czechoslovakia in February 1948 and the Russian blockade of the western sectors of the occupied city of Berlin in June of the

Trouble in Kenya; *askari* of the King's African Rifles lead packhorses along a trail in the Aberdare Mountains, during the Mau-Mau rebellion (1953).

Trouble in Korea; British soldiers race across cotton fields, bayonets fixed, near the road to Pyongyang, the North Korean capital (1950).

same year. The blockade was broken by the Allied airlift, and it may have been the presence of an American nuclear air strike force in England that dissuaded the Russians from using their overwhelming military strength in an attack on western Europe. One result of the Berlin Blockade was the signing of the North Atlantic Treaty in April 1949 which, for the first time, brought America directly into the framework of European defence.

The next Communist move was made in Korea. It was countered by the Americans who, on the orders of President Truman and under the command of General MacArthur, checked the Communist invasion of South Korea and drove it back. In July 1951 a Commonwealth Division was formed at Tokchong when, in a brief ceremony, the flags of Great Britain, Canada, Australia, New Zealand and India were broken together. This division fought alongside the Americans throughout the Korean War which, after the intervention of an enormous, ill-equipped army of Chinese 'volunteers', took on all the less desirable characteristics of an ideological struggle. Commonwealth prisoners of war were treated abominably and subjected to intensive indoctrination with the object of converting them to Communism. Few British soldiers are politically minded, and a combination of their lack of interest in the subject and sense of humour which seems to be stimulated by misfortune made the task of the Chinese very hard. They took their revenge in brutal treatment and the conditioning of their prisoners by every form of physical and psychological pressure. Several George Crosses were awarded for extreme gallantry in captivity.

In the period from the end of the Second World War until 1967 the British army was called upon to undertake peace-keeping operations at various times in the Gold Coast, British Honduras, Hong Kong, Aden, the Cameroons, Nassau, Jamaica, Kuwait, Zanzibar, Tanganyika, Uganda and Mauritius, in addition to the major operations in Palestine, Malaya, Kenya, Cyprus and Korea, and against the Indonesians in Borneo and Sarawak. Operations such as the war in Malaya involved all three Services. The Royal Navy blockaded the coasts and cut the Communist terrorists off from external aid, the Royal Air Force perfected the techniques of air supply and tactical air support to long-range patrols in the jungle, and the army outwitted and outfought the terrorists at their own game. As a result, Britain was able to place the independence of Malaya in the hands of a democratic and friendly government.

While the army was coping with all these emergencies in various parts of the world the British Army of the Rhine still had to be kept up to strength and trained for quite a different sort of major defensive war in Europe. Thus throughout the 1950s, while the Empire, in the military phrase, was 'running down', the army was stretched to the limit. Indeed from 1945 onwards it had been clear that the forces needed to deal with the problems which had arisen largely because of the war could not be maintained by the normal peacetime methods of recruiting, and there could be no question yet of doing away with conscription. The burden of running down the Empire therefore fell mainly on the shoulders of the citizen army, the National Service force of young men conscripted at first for two years and then for eighteen months. The pattern of their unenviable

Trouble in Malaya; a patrol in the jungle.

Trouble in Aden; mine clearance in the Radfan.

Training in Berlin in 1965; seventeen years earlier the Allied airlift had broken the Russian blockade of the city.

task seldom differed. The round of terrorism, intimidation, murder, arson, ambushes and bombings seemed to be endlessly repeated in the various emergencies.

The fiasco of the Suez operation in 1956 was not the fault of the soldiers who, at such short notice, had to translate into terms of military action the dithering of a British Prime Minister who had given the Egyptian government every warning of his plans, and had at the same time managed to align the whole body of world opinion against Britain and France. The Suez adventure underlined the unpalatable fact that Britain was no longer a major world power, for world power has always depended primarily on a country's economic resources and political strength. Britain had neither at the time of Suez.

As the Empire dwindled away, strategic planning centred on the nuclear deterrent. Forces were reduced: conscription was abolished in 1960. Trouble in what was left of the Empire would be dealt with by a strategic reserve organized and equipped on an 'airportable' basis operating from the United Kingdom. With a sigh of relief the regular army shrugged off the burden of National Service training and was thankful to be once more a force of efficient professionals. Yet the close contact with the citizen army which had lasted for twenty years had brought about one major change. The gap between the nation and its army had been bridged: no longer was there any social barrier between the soldier and the civilian, simply because so many civilians had been soldiers.

Suez; Colonel P. E. Crook
(3rd Para.) and his troops
advance to occupy
buildings at El Gamil Airport
just after landing (1956).

The army after 1960 was infinitely more professional in terms of skill, enthusiasm and technique than it had ever been before. Command of a battalion was now looked upon as a mere step in an officer's career; previously it had been the high peak of ambition. Many old traditions and loyalties were ruthlessly broken down in a series of amalgamations which sometimes united highly disparate regiments; but it was generally accepted that the concept of an amorphous 'Corps of Infantry', with numbered regiments, must be avoided at all costs, even though all regiments had been proud of their numbers only eighty years before.

The scale of amalgamations increased. Hybrids were grafted on to hybrids and the original structure of 'large regiments', called 'brigades' for convenience, was whittled down into a divisional organization which has much in common with Wellington's Peninsular Army. He had four infantry divisions, one Light Division and the regiments of the Guards, originally brought into the establishment by Charles II. The shrinking process applied to the army, gradually at first after 1945, and then with ever-increasing pressure, had in fact produced four infantry divisions, one Light Division and the Guards, together with certain other formations which Wellington could never have foreseen. Thus in the 1970s the army consists of the Guards Division, which is really the old 'Brigade', the Scottish Division, The Queen's Division, The King's Division, The Prince of Wales's Division, and The Light Division. The 'Horse' is grouped in the Household Cavalry and the Royal Armoured Corps, and in addition there are the Brigade of Gurkhas, The Parachute Regiment and the Special Air Service Regiment.

These divisional and formation groupings are purely administrative. In battle their units fight within the normal Corps, Divisional and Brigade staff organization, but as battle groups and combat teams. These are carefully balanced, mobile and immensely hard-hitting forces of all arms, as flexible as anything Rommel ever devised, closely co-ordinated and virtually self-contained.

The battle group and combat team organization is designed to cope with the problems of fast-moving operations conducted over great distances under the nuclear threat, and towards the end of the 1960s it appeared that with the handing over of Malaya, the reduction of the forces in Singapore and the withdrawal from the Middle East (except for the small sovereign base areas in Cyprus) it might be possible for the army to concentrate on its role in support of the nuclear deterrent. The murders, the bombings, the constant and depressing efforts to combat terrorism in the former possessions along the Imperial lifelines seemed to have come to an end. But it was at this moment that the Irish chose to revive the age-old insoluble Irish Problem, the conflict between the Catholics who desire a united, independent Ireland, and the Protestants who wish to maintain the link with Britain.

Trouble in Northern Ireland; the most unpleasant of all military duties, keeping the peace (Andersonstown, Belfast).

Men of the Royal Regiment of Wales patrolling in Northern Ireland. A picture which speaks for itself.

This, of course, is an over-simplification of a situation which has its roots in the production by Henry II, on his only visit to Ireland in the year 1171, of a Papal Bull, signed sixteen years previously by Pope Adrian – ironically enough, the only English Pope – which granted the 'overlordship of Ireland' to the English Crown. It appears now, although only on the surface, that the issue is primarily a religious one. But the history of Ireland's attempts to throw off the English yoke is long, sombre and bloody. The fearful 'rebellions' of 1641 and 1798, the massacres of Elizabeth I's wars, of Cromwell, of William III; the civil war of 1922, the troubles of 1936 and the 1950s, are all part of a history written in blood.

The role of the British army in Northern Ireland today is to try and contain the terrorism until a political solution can be found, and to prevent civil war in Ulster. It is a thankless and apparently hopeless task in which the soldiers find themselves regarded as enemies by the people they have been ordered to protect. If any solution is found, if the horrors can be brought to an end, it will not so much be the achievement of politicians as the result of the kindliness, the good humour, the patience, discipline and courage of the ordinary soldier of the British army.

Even so, he has always been regarded as one of the most formidable fighting men in the world.

'Have particular attention', wrote Louis XIV to Marshal Villeroi in 1706, 'to that part of the line which will bear the first shock of the English troops.'

BIBLIOGRAPHY

AMERY, L. S. (ed.) *The Times History of the War in South Africa*, 7 vols., London 1900–9

ANBUREY, Thomas *With Burgoyne from Quebec*, London 1963, New York 1964

ANON. *A Handbook of the Boer War*, London 1910

ANON. *Field of Mars*, 2 vols., London 1805

ANTON, Quartermaster-Sgt. James *Retrospect of Military Life*, London 1841

ATKINSON, C. T. *Marlborough and the Rise of the British Army*, New York and London 1921

BARNES, R. M. *A History of the Regiments and Uniforms of the British Army*, London and Toronto 1950

BAYNES, John *Morale; a Study of Man and Courage*, London and New York 1967

BEHRENS, C. B. A. *The Ancien Regime*, London and New York 1967

BIDDULPH, Gen. Robert *Lord Cardwell at the War Office*, London 1904

BOND, Brian (ed.) *Victorian Military Campaigns*, London and New York 1967

BRADLEY, A. G. *Fight with France for North America*, London 1900, New York 1901

CLARKE, The Rev. J. S. *The Life of James II*, London 1813

CLAUSEWITZ, Karl von *Vom Kriege*, Berlin 1880

CHURCHILL, Sir Winston *Marlborough, His Life and Times*, 6 vols., London and New York 1933–8

CORBETT, Sir J. S. *England in the Seven Years' War*, London 1908

COSTELLO, Edward *Adventures of a Soldier*, London 1852

CRUTTWELL, C. R. M. F. *A History of the Great War 1914–1918*, 2nd edn, Oxford 1936

CURLING, Henry (ed.) *Recollections of Rifleman Harris*, London 1848

DAVIS, Col. John *History of the Second Queen's*, 6 vols., London 1887–1902

DUNLOP, Col. J. K. *The Development of the British Army 1899–1914*, London and Toronto 1938

EGGENBERGER, David *A Dictionary of Battles*, London 1967

FARRER, J. A. *Military Manners and Customs*, London 1885

FARWELL, Byron *Queen Victoria's Little Wars*, London 1973

FORTESCUE, Sir John *A History of the British Army*, 13 vols., London and New York 1899–1912

FULLER, Maj.-Gen. J. F. C. *The Conduct of War, 1789–1961*, London and New Brunswick 1961

GARCIA, A. *History of the West Indies*, London 1965

GILBY, Thomas *Britain at Arms*, London 1953

GLOVER, Richard *Peninsular Preparation: the Reform of the British Army 1795–1809*, Cambridge 1963

GODWIN-AUSTEN, Maj. A. R. *The Staff and the Staff College*, London 1927

GRAVES, Robert *Sergeant Lamb of the Ninth*, London and New York 1940

GREW, E. S., *et al. Field-Marshal Lord Kitchener, His Life and Work for the Empire*, 3 vols., London 1917

HASWELL, Jock *Citizen Armies*, London 1973

HERTZ, G. B. *British Imperialism in the Eighteenth Century*, London 1908

HUTCHINSON, Lt.-Col. G. S. *The British Army*, London 1945

JACKSON, Sgt. Murray *A Soldier's Diary; South Africa, 1899–1901*, London 1913

JAMES II, King *Memoirs*, transl. by A. Lytton Sells, London and Bloomington 1962

JOHNES, Thomas (ed.) *Sir John Froissart's Chronicles*, London 1806

JOHNSTON, S. H. F. *British Soldiers*, London 1945

KINCAID, Capt. J. *Random Shots of a Rifleman*, London 1847

LAFFIN, John *Tommy Atkins; the Story of the English Soldier*, London 1966, New York 1967

LIDDELL HART, Sir Basil *A History of the World War*, London 1934

LONGFORD, Lady Elizabeth *Wellington, The Years of the Sword*, London and New York 1969

LUVAAS, Jay *The Education of an Army; British Military Thought, 1815–1940*, Chicago 1964, London 1965

MORAN, Lord *The Anatomy of Courage*, London and Toronto 1945

MORRIS, Donald R. *The Washing of the Spears*, New York 1965, London 1966

NAPIER, Sir W. F. P. *History of the War in the Peninsula*, 7 vols., London 1851

OMAN, Sir Charles *Wellington's Army 1809–1814*, London 1912

PARES, R. *War and Trade in the West Indies 1739–1763*, Oxford 1936

PARKMAN, Francis *France and England in North America*, selections by S. E. Morison, Boston 1955, London 1956

RAMSAY, David *The History of the American Revolution*, London 1791

ROBERTSON, Field-Marshal Sir William *From Private to Field-Marshal*, London and Boston 1921

SCOULLER, Maj. R. E. *The Armies of Queen Anne*, Oxford 1966

SELIMAN, R. R. *Medieval English Warfare*, London and Toronto 1960

SHEPPARD, E. W. *A Short History of the British Army*, London 1926

SLIM, Field-Marshal Viscount *Defeat into Victory*, London 1956

STEVENSON, J. *A Soldier in Time of War*, Edinburgh 1841

STOCQUELER, J. H. *The British Soldier*, London 1857

TRANT, T. A. *Two Years in Ava*, London 1827

WARD, S. G. P. *Wellington's Headquarters*, Oxford 1957

WATTEVILLE, Col. H. de *The British Soldier*, London 1954, New York 1955

WHEELER, Capt. O. *The War Office, Past and Present*, London 1914

WILLIAMSON, James A. *A Short History of British Expansion*, London 1945

WINSTOCK, Lewis *Songs and Music of the Redcoats 1642–1902*, London 1970

LIST OF ILLUSTRATIONS